PARANORMAL

PRIMER

Raymond Buckland

QVP
Queen Victoria Press

PARANORMAL PRIMER

ISBN 978-0-9978481-4-4

The majority of this work was previously published in 1969 under the title *A Pocket Guide to the Supernatural*

Queen Victoria Press
153 East South Street, Ste. 892
Wooster, OH 44691-0892

CONTENTS

INTRODUCTION

There are many people who have used a "talking board" but have never used a pendulum; have attended a séance but have never seen a ghost; have had their palms read but have never seen a deck of tarot cards. There are many, many more people who have done none of these things but would dearly love to . . . if only they knew how. Now perhaps they can. At least they can try. *Paranormal Primer* is a how-to-do-it book for those who wish to experiment with the unknown.

Under the heading TALKING BOARD, for example, will be found explicit instructions on how to operate such a board, the types of questions to ask, the number of people that may use it at one time, how to cross-reference, check results, messages, etc., etc. Full details so that anyone who has never used one before may now do so. There will even be found instructions on how to make your own fully operative board. Equally comprehensive instructions are to be found for the pendulum, the tarot cards, I-Ching, table-tipping, and many more.

Many fascinating aspects of the supernatural have had to be omitted through lack of space and by virtue of being beyond practicability for the man in the street. Other aspects are mentioned briefly—déjà vu and ectoplasm, for example—to help towards a better understanding of the subjects dealt with in depth. In no way does this book pretend to be a fully comprehensive occult dictionary. It is, as its title suggests, a pocket guide and instruction book which should prove equally valuable to both beginner and advanced student of parapsychology.

The author has obtained knowledge of the various contents through his own experiences and the experiences of other serious investigators. It is hoped that readers will not hesitate to document their own experiences.

RAYMOND BUCKLAND

I

ASTRAL PROJECTION

The body as we know it has an invisible double—known variously as the spirit, ethereal body, astral body. It is an exact duplicate of its physical counterpart though, as will be seen, there are occasions when it may temporarily change its shape. It is this astral body which acts as your "stand-in" in your dreams. There are a number of methods that may be used to enable you to consciously travel with this astral body and we will deal with one or two of them here.

All people dream, though not everyone remembers the dream. Frequently dreams seem ridiculously mixed-up. This is because you are only remembering the highlights of a number of dreams; for the average person experiences quite a number in one period of sleep. Suppose that in the dream state—or, more correctly, on the Astral Plane—you take a trip to Scotland and go salmon fishing. From there you travel to the Orient for a pleasant trip in a sampan. Then you may have a dream of visiting the pyramids in Egypt, and round off the night refighting the Civil War. On waking you may only have a confused recollection of what seemed like one strange dream, where you were drifting down the Nile in a chinese junk which suddenly disappeared and left you fighting the whole of the Confederate Army armed with nothing but a salmon-fishing rod!

The first step, then, is to teach yourself to remember all the details of all your dreams. This will take time but is not difficult. All you have to do is to keep a notebook and a pen or pencil beside your bed and, *immediately on waking*, write down all that you can remember of what you have dreamt. Initially you may remember nothing at all; but keep trying. You may get jumbled impressions as above. Slowly but surely they will become less jumbled. Eventually you will remember all details of each individual dream. I know a woman who is able to wake up periodically throughout the night, write down her dream, then go back to sleep for the next dream.

The next step is to decide before going to sleep just what dream you would like to have. Make a note in your book; perhaps, "Will go to Boston; see the grave of Cotton Mather; visit the old North Church, where Paul Revere hung his lanterns."

Then go to sleep keeping these directions firmly in your mind. If you are planning to go somewhere you have been before, imagine yourself going over the route to get there, as you fall asleep. See yourself leaving your house; driving along the Parkway; noticing any special landmarks. As usual, on waking, note the details of your dreams.

You may have missed, however and you may have gone nowhere near Boston. Don't be discouraged; just keep trying. Eventually you will be able to direct yourself where you wish.

Using the above example, suppose you did dream of going to Boston and visiting the sights. If you have never been there in real life then the following day check on the details you noted from your dream. The overall appearance of the old North Church will be easily confirmed from photographs. Check photographs and reference books for the other smaller details in your notebook. You will be surprised to find that they all check out. Here will be proof that your astral body really did make the journey. You will by now notice that you are actually *living* the dream. Rather than a blank period of sleep followed by remembrance of the dreams, you will feel that you are actually there at the time, participating.

Let us go a step further. You now have pretty much control of yourself on the Astral Plane. At some point in your dream stop yourself and decide to go back and look at your sleeping, physical body. You will find yourself in your bedroom, standing beside the bed looking down at an inert figure that looks exactly like you. That the room is in darkness does not matter; you will see everything perfectly well. You will feel that the astral you is the *real* you and that the figure in the bed is just a shell. You may—though not everybody can—see a fine, silver thread, or cord, connecting your astral body to your physical body. This is incredibly elastic. Wherever your astral body goes the cord will stretch. It is your life-line and is responsible for pulling you back to your body in case of emergency. Any sort of interruption to your sleep, such as the alarm clock going off, will cause your immediate return, no matter how far away you are. It is this silver cord which, at the time of death, finally severs from the physical body and allows the astral body, or spirit, to go on.

Another method of astral projection is the induced trance. This can be done at almost any time since you do not actually go to sleep, in the strict sense of the word. It is the hazy borderline between waking and sleeping, and with a little practice can be fairly readily attained. It helps to be well rested—so that you do not fall into a deep, natural, sleep—and also to have recently fed well. Choose a time, and place, where you can have absolute quiet. No radios and televisions heard dimly in the background; no sound at all. Lie in the most comfortable position—on your back, on your side; it does not matter which—on a settee or bed and let your eyelids close. Relax and breathe deeply and evenly. Relaxation and deep, regular, breathing are very important. Lie there and imagine your whole body relaxing, by degrees. Think to yourself, "My feet are relaxing; they are relaxing; they are completely at ease. My legs are relaxing. They are warm and comfortable; completely relaxed; completely at rest. . . ." Continue with all the limbs; the whole body. Breathe deeply and regularly all the time.

When all the body has been covered in this way, and you are completely at ease, then—with your eyes still closed—start to think of your surroundings. The settee, or bed, on which you are lying. The rug. The curtains at the window. The first few times you try absolutely nothing may happen. Eventually, however, you will find that you will be able to see the room around you, even though your eyes are closed. Just lie and imagine the room; think of the positions of the furniture, the patterns on the wallpaper and upholstery. Suddenly you will realize that, rather than imagining, you are actually looking at these things.

At this stage, or even slightly before, you may feel a strange sensation—a numbness that starts at your feet and gradually moves up through your whole body. This sensation is actually the separating of your Astral body from your Physical body. You will have absolutely no wish whatsoever to move. You may think to yourself that, if you wanted to, you could lift an arm, or move a leg, but you just can't be bothered. All that is necessary now is to will yourself to leave your body and you will drift out of it. You will be able to stand up, beside your physical body.

It sometimes happens that, as you lie on your settee, relaxing and breathing deeply, you will get a sudden feeling that your eyes are rolling upwards. It is almost as though you are looking up and back into your own brain; towards the pineal gland. You may then get a sensation of rushing upwards, towards the top of your head, until you suddenly find yourself standing, calmly and in peace, beside your own self. This is known as exiting by the Pineal Door (or Pineal Door projection). It does not often happen but do not be afraid if it does.

Should you ever be in a state of partial release do not worry. Partial release is when you feel your astral self is almost ready to leave the body but not quite. You may lift your (astral) arms but feel that the rest of you is tied down. Just relax and tell yourself that if your arms are ready, so is the rest of you. Sit up, and stand up. You will have no problem. Alternatively think of yourself as sliding up into your head and out the Pineal Door, and that you will do.

Very probably when you first leave your body you will experience dual consciousness. You will feel yourself in your astral body, standing up, but at the same time you will feel yourself in your physical body, lying down. Just concentrate on the "you" in the astral body and go on your way. The physical feeling will disappear.

Another excellent way of experiencing astral projection is via the "False Awakening." Most people have had the experience of half waking in the morning and knowing, or being told, that it is time to get up out of bed and get dressed. They get out of bed and sleepily start to dress. They may ponder what to wear, reach a decision, and then dress fully. Suddenly the alarm clock goes off again, or someone calls, and—surprise—they realize they are still lying in bed! Yet they would have sworn they actually got up and got dressed. This was the Astral body that acted out the getting up. And if you can realize that it is only your Astral acting, then you can carry on from there.

You can go, on the Astral Plane, virtually anywhere. Then when you return you will go back into your physical body and wake up in the normal manner. It is just recognizing of the False Awakening for what it is, that is the difficult part. The only way is to look out for falsities—things which, although they seem absolutely real, obviously could not be. You might "wake up" and, as you are getting dressed, notice a suit of armor standing in the corner. You know you do not own a suit of armor yet it, and the whole scene, seems absolutely real. Concentrate, then, on making the armor disappear. It will eventually do so, and that is your confirmation that you are on the Astral.

The Astral Plane can be anything, as can you. It usually looks like your everyday surroundings because that's what you know best. In the same way, you know yourself best as you are. But if you wished, you could change things. Think of yourself with red hair, and you *have* red hair. Think of yourself as being just that little bit taller you've always wished you were—and you are. Think of yourself sitting in a restaurant halfway around the world, and you are there. Immediately. More from habit than anything you will open doors to go through them, but this is not necessary. You can *think* yourself through them; float through like the proverbial "ghost." Actually when you seemingly open a door, on the Astral Plane, it is only an astral door, for you cannot affect the material world. You cannot actually move real objects and you cannot, with one exception, be seen by other physical bodies. The exception is, people who are sensitives, who have a certain psychic ability. These are the people who see "ghosts" —and indeed many so-called ghosts are only the materialized, or partially materialized, astral bodies of persons sleeping or entranced elsewhere.

There are other ways of inducing Astral Projection (through hypnosis, for example) but the above are the easiest, and safest, methods for the beginner. Not everyone can have success. Or, more correctly, not everyone can have memory of their astral travels. However a large number can, and you may be in that number. Do not forget to write down all your experiences, whether they work out well, or badly. Whatever the occult field, *always* keep careful notes.

14

II

ASTROLOGY

Astrology is perhaps one of the most popular of the occult sciences; the one most used by "the man in the street." Although staunchly denying any serious belief in such matters nine out of ten persons are unable to read a daily newspaper or monthly magazine without avidly scanning the horoscopes to see what the day/ week/month holds in store for them. It is useless to point out to these people that the majority of these horoscopes are, by virtue of their generality, completely worthless. In what follows will be seen the elements that make a true horoscope a very personal thing, applicable only to the one for whom it is cast.

The individual horoscope, or natal chart—the one that interprets the motions of the heavenly bodies in terms of the person's life—comes under the awesome-sounding heading of *genethliacal* astrology. The chart is actually a map of how the planets, Sun and Moon, appear at the moment of birth.

Each planet has a particular influence on the person born and also a particular influence on the other planets, depending on its proximity. To erect, or draw up, this chart for the individual certain things must be known. Firstly, the *date* of birth—day, month, year. Secondly, the *place* of birth—geographical location. And thirdly, the *time* of birth—the actual hour, preferably to the nearest minute. Why are all these things necessary? From the Earth the Sun seems to describe a great circle in its travels. This path is called the *Ecliptic,* and the angle that it makes at any moment, as it rises above the eastern horizon, is called the *Ascendant.* This name, Ascendant,

15

is also given to the sign of the Zodiac that is rising at a given time. A different ascending sign appears over the horizon *every four minutes*. It can therefore be seen that to obtain the correct sign and ecliptic, at the moment of birth, the time and place of birth must be accurately recorded.

As the Sun moves throughout the year it passes through twelve different areas of sky and constellations. These are the *Houses* of the Zodiac and, like the hand of the watch, sweeps round. The dividing lines between the Houses are known as *Cusps*. The Sun takes roughly a month to pass through each of the Houses, which are as follows:

ARIES — March 21 through April 19

TAURUS — April 20 through May 19

GEMINI — May 20 through June 20

CANCER — June 21 through July 22

LEO — July 23 through August 21

VIRGO — August 22 through September 22

LIBRA — September 23 through October 22

SCORPIO — October 23 through November 21

SAGITTARIUS — November 22 through December 21

CAPRICORN — December 22 through January 20

AQUARIUS — January 21 through February 19

PISCES — February 20 through March 20

In planning this map of the heavens some help is needed in establishing the positions held by the planets at the many different hours and minutes that have passed with the years. The Astrologer's aids for this are the *Ephemeris* and the *Table of Houses*. The Ephemeris gives the positions of the planets at the different times while the Table of Houses gives the corrections with regard to the place of birth; the geographical location. Measurement of time is given in what is known as *sidereal time,* measured by the stars rather than the Sun. The stars appear to move around the sky at a faster rate than the Sun, and this must be allowed for in the calculation of sidereal time.

Working, then, from the Ephemeris you must first calculate the sidereal time (shown as S.T.) at the moment of birth. If born before noon the necessary hours and minutes will be subtracted from the S.T. given for noon in the Ephemeris. If born after noon the hours and minutes will be added to the S.T. given in the Ephemeris. And just to round things off nicely, an extra ten seconds per hour (known as the *acceleration on interval*) must also be subtracted or added. With a person born, for example, in New York further adjustment would be necessary since most Ephemerides use G.M.T. as standard. (e.g. 5:45 P.M. in New York would be 10:45 P.M. at G.M.T.)

EXAMPLE: A person born at 11:45 A.M. on August 31st, 1934, in New York, would have the S.T. 10 hrs 35 mins 54 secs. (4:45 P.M. at G.M.T.) The acceleration on interval would be 10 times 4¾ (hours after noon) seconds. The S.T. for the moment of birth would then be:

	10h	35m	54s
+	4h	45m	0s
+			48s
	15h	21m	42s

The next step would then be to convert this G.M.T.-S.T. to New York-S.T. by conversion of the degrees and minutes of longitude into minutes and seconds of time. This can be done by simply multiplying by four and *adding* if the location is east of Greenwich, or *subtracting* if west of Greenwich. In the above example, New York is 74° west of Greenwich. Multiply by four and subtract from the S.T.:

```
15h   21m   42s
- 4h   56m   0s
```

```
10h   25m   42s   =   local S.T. for New York.
```

From longitude the move is a natural one to latitude. From the Table of Houses can be found the ascendants for the local S.T. just calculated. The latitude for New York is 40°43′ N. (North of the Equator). Looking at the Table of Houses for New York, then, you would find:

S.T.			ASC.		
h	m	s	°	♏	′
10	25	42	22	35	

22°35′ Scorpio.

Now, at last, you can start to fill in one of those fascinating horoscope blanks. A line may be drawn, through the center, connecting the degree of the ascendant on one side of the chart with a point exactly opposite on the other side. This point opposite is called the *Descendant*. Also in the Table of Houses will be found the related *medium coeli* (M.C.)—its opposite point is the *imum coeli* (I.C.)—the mid-point at right angles to the connected Ascendant and Descendant. These lines/points are also marked on the chart. The chart is now divided into its four quadrants.

The next stage in drawing the "map" is the filling-in of the "house boundaries." The Ascendant is the start of the first house and from there will be found twelve houses (see figure 1).

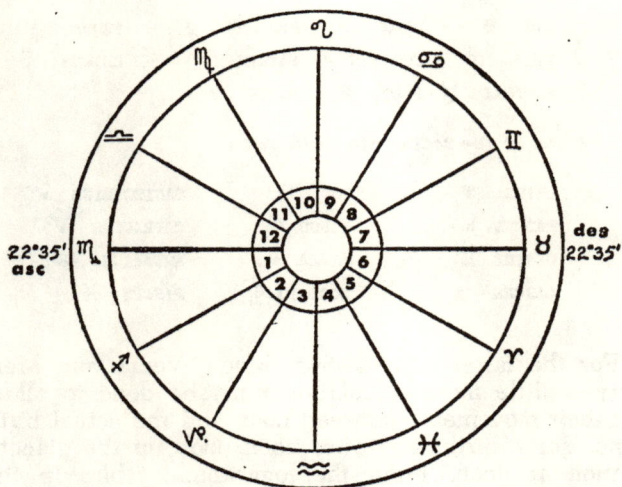

Fig.1

The positions of the Sun, Moon and the planets are found thus: from the Ephemeris find the positions for noon, on the birth day, of Saturn, Neptune, Jupiter, Uranus and Pluto. These are the slower planets. These positions can be put straight on to the chart. They are shown, as are all planets, on the chart and in the tables, by their signs. These traditional signs are:

SUN	☉	MOON	☽	MERCURY	☿	VENUS	♀
MARS	♂	JUPITER	♃	SATURN	♄	URANUS	♅
NEPTUNE	♆	PLUTO	♇	EARTH	○		

The Signs of the Zodiao are shown thus:

ARIES	♈	LEO	♌	SAGITTARIUS	♐
TAURUS	♉	VIRGO	♍	CAPRICORN	♑
GEMINI	♊	LIBRA	♎	AQUARIUS	♒
CANCER	♋	SCORPIO	♏	PISCES	♓

For the faster planets—Sun, Moon, Venus and Mercury—a little more calculation must be done to allow for their movements between noon and the actual birth time. For a birth time after noon, look up the planet's motion at noon. From the logaritnmic tables in the Ephemeris find the log. of the motion and to it add the log. of the interval after noon (a birth time of 6:30 P.M. would give an interval of six and a half hours). Then convert the total log. back to degrees. You now have the difference in position of the planet at noon on the birth date and can add this to the noon position the Ephemeris shows. Had the actual birth time been *before* noon, then you would have looked up the planet's motion at noon on the day *before* the actual birth date and proceeded as above. Should the planet in question be marked "R" in the tables—meaning that it is retrograde—then you would subtract the movement on interval from the noon position. One word of warning—do not forget to convert Greenwich S.T. to local S.T. when filling in the positions of the planets. A chart at this stage may look like this:

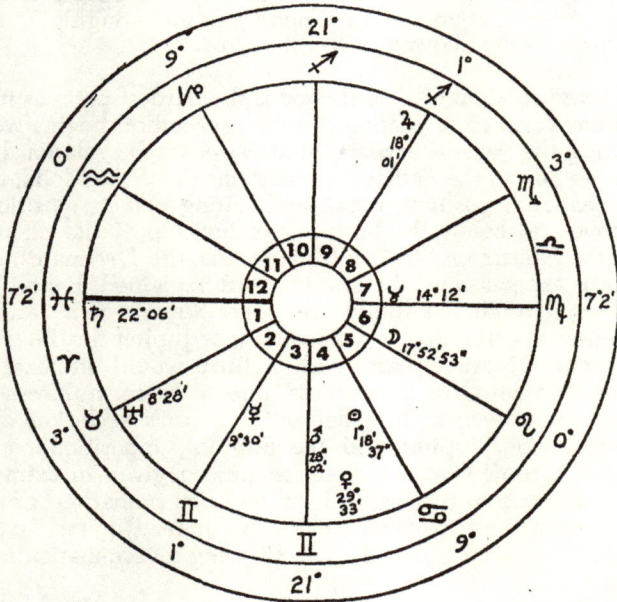

Fig. 2

Before you can attempt to interpret a horoscope you must know what the various positions of the planets mean in relation to one another; their *Aspects*. Two planets, one rising and the other setting, 180° apart, are said to be in *Opposition*. This is traditionally a bad aspect. Two planets within approximately 10° of each other are in *Conjunction*, which can be either good or bad depending on which the planets are. Planets 90°

21

apart are said to be *Square,* another bad aspect; while 60° apart (*Sextile*) is a good aspect. Finally, of the main aspects, 120° apart is extremely good and goes by the name - *Trine.* Obviously in these positions a certain amount of leeway is permissible and this is usually in the order of 10° to 12° for Conjunction or Opposition, and roughly 7° for Sextile. These allowances are the *Orbs.*

Interpretation of a horoscope is the hardest part—as it is in any form of divination. The interpretation begins with listing the various aspects which appear; the relationship of the Sun to the Zodiac; the relationship of the Moon; the Ascendant's position; rising and setting planets; positions above and below the horizon; relationship of the planets to the Houses and to the Zodiac signs; the Decanates. All these aspects must be studied and explained. Examples of what might be found are: Mars Square with Saturn, Jupiter and the Sun in Opposition, or Jupiter Sextile with Mercury. Mars Square with Saturn would indicate a certain amount of callousness, due to Mars' ruthlessness and impulsiveness together with Saturn's seclusion and introversion. Jupiter and the Sun in Opposition could mean a somewhat self-centered person given to extrav—agance, due to the forcefulness and determination of the Sun with the expansive wealth of Jupiter. Jupiter Sextile with Mercury would be good, showing determination and knowledge with judgment.

The planets themselves have certain qualities: Air, Water, Fire or Earth. Traditionally Gemini, Aquarius, and Libra are the Air signs; Cancer, Scorpio, and Pisces the Water signs; Aries, Leo, and Sagittarius the Fire signs, and Taurus, Virgo and Capricorn the Earth signs. Air signs are supposedly intellectual, enlightened, and articulate; watery signs emotional; fiery signs zealous and fervent; earthy signs cautious, basic, practical. In more detail the signs — again, *by tradition,* as is almost all interpretation in astrology — are associated with particular

22.

attributes. ARIES is very much a leader or pioneer. There is a certain amount of impatience in this sign, due to ambition. TAURUS is the hard worker: great strength, and proud of it, along with perseverance.

GEMINI is adaptable; knows a little about a lot of subjects, has a gift for languages, diplomacy and tact, but is somewhat superficial. CANCER is extremely sensitive, a follower of tradition, a great homelover. LEO is the extrovert— full of self-confidence, and has an abundance of personality, a great sense of the dramatic, and a great capacity for love.

VIRGO is the critic — tidy and conservative, yet always charming and popular, Virgo is the best of planners and organizers, intellectual, and extremely analytical. LIBRA has intuition and foresight, is peace-loving and has a great sense of justice. SCORPIO has tenacity and determination, great self-control but a rather too fine opinion of himself. At times he seems a contradiction to himself—jealous and demanding. SAGITTARIUS knows no fear. Kind and can be gentle, he is also direct and outspoken. CAPRICORN is ambitious and very materialistic, has a fear of inadequacy and indigence, and is either greatly depressed or incredibly happy. AQUARIUS is a planner, always looking ahead: honest, kind, yet difficult to understand. Independent in the extreme, he has very good judgment. PISCES is sensitive, noble, kind and gentle, yet can be vague and inclined to be too optimistic. Self-sacrificing and sympathetic, Pisces is an excellent diplomat.

SATURN is inhibited, persevering, cautious and often frustrated, taciturn, reserved. Saturn is associated with the law, mining, printing, dentistry, building and real estate, second-hand goods, agriculture and death. URANUS is excitable and erratic, a little too forceful, and inclined to be sarcastic. It has an affinity with nature, also technical objects. To do with electricians, inventors, and astrologers.

Very much of the occult. NEPTUNE is inclined to mysticism, also to individuality. Knows, but does not say. Can be of very doubtful character, capable of murder, rape, etc. Sometimes vague, sometimes confused. Associated with eating places, bars, prostitution, narcotics, navigation, the ocean, nursing, advertising.

PLUTO is generally associated with children; youth. Leaders, wanting things their own way, disliking laws. Pluto is associated with hobbies, sports, outdoor life, actors and actresses, politicians. JUPITER is the planet of harmony, of education, law, morals and religion, faith, good humor. Truth comes before anything with Jupiter. Knowledge, the ability to self-educate, learning through reading, are all of Jupiter. Moneyed people count with this planet; bankers, judges, ecclesiastics.

The SUN is first and foremost a masculine planet, full of vitality. It has determination yet much kindness, a lot of heart, and is capable of great love—an authoritative figure, moving ever forward. The MOON, conversely, is a feminine figure; very sensitive, emotional, domestic—a lover of water, patriotic and interested in public welfare. MERCURY is quick-witted—an extremely active mind, good for research, exploration, analysis, judgment; good for writers, teachers, orators. VENUS is again, of course, feminine; very much of love. To do with friendship, physical attraction, feeling, peace-making, pleasures; associated with musicians, jewelers, actors, dress-makers, artists and nurses. MARS is for action, with great energy and courage. May be brutal and may be jealous—frequently the cause of sexual problems. Impulsive; loyal; fearful of the unknown; associated with soldiers, surgeons, sportsmen and craftsmen.

Each of the twelve Zodiac signs is spoken of as being "ruled" by one of the planets. What this means is that there is a close affinity between the two. Where a planet is classed as being "watery" or "fiery," so the sign or signs that it rules are of that type. The sign Aries is ruled by the planet Mars. Taurus is ruled by Venus. Gemini by Mercury; Cancer by the Moon; Leo by the Sun; Virgo by Mercury; Libra by Venus; Scorpio by Mars; Sagittarius by Jupiter; Capricorn by Saturn; Aquarius by Saturn (some astrologers prefer Uran us); and Pisces by Jupiter (again, some say by Neptune). Generally it can be said that a fiery sign would not get along well with a water sign. Nor would a water or earth sign get along with an air sign. An air sign, however, would do well with a fire sign, and so on.

We should now look at the twelve divisions, the Spheres of Influence, on the chart and see what each is concerned with. They are numbered, on the chart. The first one is the Sphere influencing the physical appearance, the body. The second deals with money, gaining or losing, investing, etc. The third Sphere is that of communications and transportation, letters, writing and transport. Also it deals with near relatives and close neighbors. The fourth Sphere is the one of home and property. It deals with the birth place, with real estate, mines and underground places. It also deals with a man's mother or a woman's father. Pleasure—love, sex, amusement, education—appear in the fifth Sphere. Sensual pleasures especially are here. In the sixth Sphere you find health, domestic animals, and conditions effecting the health. Clothing, servants and physical comfort are also here.

The seventh Sphere of Influence shows, in a woman's chart, the husband; in a man's, the wife. Partners, generally, are here. In the eighth Sphere are losses, including death. Loss of money and possessions is here; also details of wills and legacies. The ninth Sphere covers religion, spiritual things, journeys to other lands, and relatives by marriage. The tenth Sphere covers your job, your business affairs, honors, earnings. The eleventh Sphere covers your friends and acquaintances, hopes and fears, and wishes. The twelfth Sphere of Influence shows any confinement you may encounter—prison, deportation, exile. It shows enemies and also, strangely, large animals.

From the above, then, you can really start on inter-pretation. For example: Pisces on the Ascendant. This first House deals with the physical appearance. Pisces —sensitive, noble, kind and gentle—indicates that the person will be of short to middle stature, of pale complexion, with high cheekbones, light hair and eyes. In the sixth House you find the Moon. The sixth Sphere, you know, is the one of health and physical comfort. The Moon is sensitive, emotional. You could say, then, that the person might be prone to emotional upsets; nervous breakdowns. They might also enjoy serving others, since the House also deals with servants. In the ninth House is Jupiter, the planet of harmony. He deals, as you have seen, with education and religion. The ninth House, in which he appears, is the one covering religion and spiritual things. This must signify great success for the person in religious affairs; also in philosophical and legal affairs, since Jupiter also deals with these. The interpretation would follow around taking the Houses one after the other. Then the aspects, which you listed, would be interpreted according to the associ- ations for the various planets.

It may be seen from the above, then, that although some very general characteristics might be immediately given for a person born at a particular time of year, certainly no great and accurate details can be given without having more information on both the birth time *and the birth place,* and constructing a natal chart—the map of the planets at that time and place of birth.

I have talked of a natal chart, a horoscope of the time of birth, showing what the life will hold in general. Similar charts can be made for practically any purpose. They can be plotted to show what might be the influences for a particular year, or other period of time. They can be plotted for countries, or towns, rather than for individuals. They can be plotted to show the most propitious time for laying the cornerstone of a new building; for marriage; money; health; business; indeed for practically any purpose. There are many thousands of businessmen who have a professional astrologer draw up a chart for the coming business year, and follow its indications scrupulously. They return year after year and seem more than satisfied. They take their horoscopes seriously, as they should be taken if the astrologer really knows his job.

When a daily newspaper's horoscope says that Monday morning is going to seem long and wearing to all persons born between April 20 and May 20 then, al-though it may turn out to be amazingly accurate, you may rest assured that no charts were drawn, no tables consulted, no planetary positions interpreted. Yet it is this drawing, calculating, and interpreting which makes the subject so interesting. If you would like to go further into Astrology there is a bibliography to be found at the back of this book. Read, study, and happy plotting!

III

AUTOMATIC WRITING

Perhaps the best known of automatic writers was Mrs. Curran, through whom were produced the writings of Patience Worth. Mrs. Curran had no particular interest in history and had certainly never traveled to Europe, yet through her were produced volumes of seemingly authentic first-hand accounts of Elizabethan England. The style, words and phrases were all absolutely correct for the period. Experiments with automatic writing are perhaps the easiest for the beginner in the occult field since they can be done at virtually any time; while sitting talking with someone, reading a book, or even while watching television.

Many people claim that writings produced "automatically" are no more than the surfacing of the writer's unconscious mind. This may well be true in a large number of cases, but that explanation will certainly not cover all cases. For example, there are on record cases where lost articles have been recovered by means of automatic writing. Miss Grace Rosher, with a fountain pen propped lightly against her fingers, found herself writing in a strange handwriting which finally signed itself "William Crookes." On comparison it was found that the handwriting was indeed identical to that of the late Sir William Crookes, the pioneer parapsychologist. But even if much of the material you receive should seem virtually worthless, there is a good chance that a little—perhaps only a very little—will be really worthwhile. It is this little that makes the whole field of experimenting in the paranormal very much worthwhile.

The simplest way to start automatic writing is to sit down to watch television, or read a book, with a pencil in your hand and a large pad of paper on the chair beside you. Just let your hand, holding the pencil, rest on the pad and concentrate on your book or television show. Forget about the hand holding the pencil. You will be surprised to find, on glancing down after a half hour or an hour or so, that the hand you thought was inactive has actually been very busy—writing. What it has written will probably have nothing at all to do with whatever you were watching, reading or thinking. In fact it may not even be in your own handwriting!

To start with the writing may not be very legible. It takes practice—sometimes many sessions—for the writing to settle down into its particular style. There is a theory that. it is the "spirit" of a dead person that takes over the writing hand. This would seem to be born out in the case of Miss Grace Rosher, mentioned above. It would also seem to be born out in cases where different "spirits" take over one person's hand at different times, and consequently produce totally different scripts.

Do not be disappointed if you actually get no results at all the first time, or even the first few times. It may be that you are too conscious of the hand holding the pencil. Try to forget it. Just relax and enjoy whatever else you are doing; the results will come.

If there is a group of you—say six or seven—who would like to try an automatic writing "séance" it can be very easily arranged. Sit around a small table with a large pad of paper in the center. It seems to bring better results if you sit alternately male and female. Place your hands flat on the table so that your thumbs are touching each other and your little ("pinky") fingers are touching your neighbors'. Your fingers may be spread, rather than close together. One person should be appointed the "medium." He or she is the one who · will be doing the actual writing—or more correctly, through whom the writing will be done. The medium therefore will have only one hand on the table in the circle of touching fingers. His or her other hand will be in the center holding the pencil lightly on the pad. As with the Talking Board (q.v.) all those who are present should be seriously interested in getting results.

The Medium will start by writing her own name two or three times across the top of the sheet of paper. It may be that her hand will suddenly start writing other material straight away from there. If not she should let the hand stay, as relaxed as possible while still holding the pencil, on the pad and ask, "Is there anyone here, please?" You may have to wait anything up to fifteen minutes before getting any response, repeating the question from time to time. Eventually the Medium will feel as though her hand is shaking with "nerves." She will perhaps just scribble wavy lines across the page without being able to help herself. The wavy lines will soon turn into words. Again they may not be too legible at first but will eventually settle into regular handwriting.

The writing may just keep going, probably filling pages and pages of paper, till the Medium's arm is tired. Alternatively it may just write a name—probably unknown to those present—and then stop. If this is the case the Medium may then ask questions—again as in the Talking Board experiments—and the answers will appear in writing.

An alternate method of writing is to use a *planchette*. This is easy enough to make. It is a small piece of wood which may be circular (about six to eight inches in diameter), square, triangular, or indeed practically any shape. It rests on three feet; the two rear ones being small ball-bearing type casters, and the front one being the point of a pencil or ball-point pen sticking through a hole in the wood. Consequently if the planchette is placed on a sheet of paper it is able to roll in any direction and produce a pencil or ink line. In a séance as above the Medium would be resting her hand lightly on the planchette rather than holding a pencil. The planchette would then glide about and produce the writing.

Should there be only three or four people in the group instead of making a circle of hands around the table they may each put a finger or two *lightly* on the edge of the planchette. The Medium then acts as Spokesman and, with everyone's fingers on it, the planchette produces the writing.

Checking the information obtained can be as interesting as the actual receipt of the writing. A typical list of questions to ask is given in the article on the Talking Board. These questions may be used equally well in automatic writing and similarly checked out. There is the added attraction, however, of being able to check on the handwriting. Suppose, for example, that you contact the supposed "spirit" of your Great Aunt Clara. It is more than likely that somewhere in the family there is still in existence an example of Great Aunt Clara's handwriting. Compare the two. Who knows —they may turn out to be identical!

IV

BLACK MAGIC

Black Magic may seem a strange subject to find in a "How to do it" book—even such a book as this one—but I feel it should be included if only to give a greater understanding of the beliefs behind its practice. A word of warning, however. It is one thing, to know the mechanics of a fire-arm. It is quite another thing to take that fire-arm and—even believing you could never score a hit—point it at another person and pull the trigger.

In the popular mind Black Magic, Voodoo, Witchcraft, Diabolism are all one and the same thing. In actual fact this is far from true. They are quite separate and distinct practices and religions. Black Magic is nothing more than the working of magic—supernatural, or natural, power—for black, or evil, purposes. It can be done equally well by Christian, Jew, Mohammedan, Witch, Agnostic, Atheist, or whatever. Religion has nothing to do with it for it is purely a practice; albeit the practice of an evil, warped, mind.

One of the most common forms of Black Magic is the making of a clay, or wax, figure representing a person or thing, and then maltreating it. This form of Black Magic, and in fact most forms, comes under the general heading of *sympathetic* magic. One of the earliest examples of the use of the clay image is found back in Paleolithic times (roughly 25,000 years ago), when it was used by early Man against animals, as a means of securing food. As a charm against a human it is mentioned by the ancient Egyptians. There was a conspiracy against Ramses III, who reigned about 1200 B.C., in which a treasury official used wax dolls to try to kill the king. There is also a Greek tale of the Egyptian king Nectanebo II (350 B.C.) who fought his battles with wax figures.

From time to time throughout history mention of the wax or clay image crops up. Another such case was the plot of the Berwick "witches," lead by Francis, Earl Bothwell, against England's King James VI. There was another similar plot against Queen Elizabeth I.

As stated the image may be made of wax or clay. It could as well be of mud, soap, plasticene, or any moldable substance. Recently I saw one made with children's *Play-Dough*. While molding the figure the practitioner, or Magician, should have a good, clear picture of the victim in his mind. If he has a photograph or picture of any sort, on which he can concentrate as he works, then all the better. Whether or not the image itself bears an actual life-like resemblance is immaterial. It is the thought in the Magician's mind that directs the force. If it is possible to obtain any personal effects from the victim, such as small pieces of his clothing or, better still, nail-parings, hair clippings, saliva, etc., then the image will be that much more potent by having these effects worked into it as it is formed.

Once formed the image has to be named for the victim in a simple ritual. This ritual is performed at night, preferably during the waning of the moon. The Magician lays the image on a small table together with a lighted candle, a dish of water, a container of salt, nine new pins and a censer of burning incense. The type of incense is not too important but if you want to do the job properly then burn musk, for that is the incense frequently associated with evil. Standing, or kneeling, before the table the Black Magician takes the image in his left hand and, with his right hand, sprinkles some of the salt into the water and mixes it. He then annoints the image with the salted water. Rubbing it all over he says, "I name this image . . . . It is him in all respects. It is him through the virtues of the articles within it."

He now holds the image in the smoke rising from the censer and says, "This image is . . . . and aught that I do to it, I do to him!"

The Magician then lays the image on the table before him and concentrates intensely on it. He brings all his hatred to bear on the lump of wax before him. He must bring .himself to the pitch where, if his victim were there in the flesh, he could rush upon him and attack him physically.

Then taking the nine new pins he plunges them, one at a time, into the center of the figure with the wish, "May . . . . die of a heart attack!" (or whatever dire fate he wishes). He repeats the wish with each thrust of a fresh pin. And here another warning—*once in the figure, the pins must not be touched.* As the pins are inserted should the Magician inadvertently touch one of the pins already there . . . the whole curse will come back on *him!*

Death is not necessarily the outcome desired. The pins may all be stuck into the figure's head with a wish ranging anywhere from that victim should suffer mild headaches to that he should go completely insane. Pins themselves are not always necessary. Should the desire be for the victim to break a leg then, after naming the figure and concentrating on it, the Magician fiercely makes his wish and actually snaps the leg of the waxen figure. A long, lingering illness that will cause the poor unfortunate to waste away? Simply hold the figure over the candle flame and gradually melt it. This can be done over a long period of time; melting a little each night, if necessary.

A variation on the wax figure is to take a sheep's heart and, in the same way as above, name it for the intended victim and then stick it. This is a favorite of primitive Man who will stick the heart with thorns in lieu of pins. A further variation might be to take a thin sheet of copper foil. With some scissors or shears a simple gingerbread-type figure is cut out. Again a clear picture of the victim must be in the operator's mind while cutting. After the naming and concentration the figure is then laid down and pounded with a hammer! I recently heard of this being done against someone and a few days later the victim, by a strange coincidence (?), got into a fight in a bar and was severely beaten.

The Modoc Indians, among others, used what they called "death needles" against their enemies. These look like fine slivers of mica. Against individual enemies they would make an image of beeswax and stick it with the needles. But they would also use them against a rival tribe as a whole. To do this they would catch the animal or bird that was the *totem* of the rival tribe. For example, a beaver. With great ceremony, probably including dancing around the animal, they would stick the needles into the beaver while it was still alive. Then they would let it go. This worked very "bad medicine" against the beaver tribe. The needles themselves are not poisonous. It was the whole ceremony—the working of the sympathetic magic—that did the trick. The dancing, as with the Magician's concentration, brought them to the pitch of hate (the *ekstasis*) that was necessary to produce the "power" to work that magic.

Yet another variation is the cloth figure for, as stated, virtually any material can be used. Shortly after World War II a number of figures came to light (some of them now exhibited at the Black Magic Museum, Gloucester, England) which had probably been designed to do away with the unwanted figure in a wartime love triangle. One such was a doll dressed as a Red Cross nurse—with a large, old-fashioned, hat pin through the heart. Another, similarly impaled, was a male figure in Royal Air Force uniform. Whether anyone ever tried this type of magic on the irate, little black-moustached figure in German uniform I do not know.

No cloth available? No wax, clay, soap, or any other workable material to hand? No matter, you can still create havoc with your "friends" and acquaintances! If you have a photograph of your victim then work directly on that. Stick it with pins; burn it; bang it; bury it. Whatever takes your fancy. No photograph? Then draw a sketch of him. No good at drawing? Then, as pretty much a last resort, just write the victim's name on a slip of paper. This last is not likely to be as effective as the other methods though it certainly is used and has been known to work.

What goes for humans goes just as well for animals, or even for inanimate objects. The cow will run dry of milk, the hen stop laying, even the farmer's tractor stop running if the Magician knows what he is about. A sharp pin in a suitably "consecrated" model car will give your neighbor a flat tire. A picture burned in a candle flame may cause a tube in his color television to burn out. All this malevolence, and more, is possible —if the Magician is sufficiently incensed.

And what works for evil works equally well for good. The opposite of Black Magic is, of course, White Magic. Wax figures can have broken sections molded together to help heal real broken limbs. Cloth figures can be filled with healing herbs and literally sewn up to help in the undergoing of and recovering from an operation. (There is such a figure in the Buckland Museum of Witchcraft and Magic, Cleveland, Ohio.) Even hair has been known to grow after a kindly (White) Magician suitably re-touched the photograph of a balding friend, in a ritual! Sympathetic magic has been used for many things besides the working of evil. To bring rain, when needed, a Magician would go to a stream and beat the waters with a broom. This caused the water to splash up in the air and fall again, like rain. Like attracts like, was the belief.

Just how does this magic work? Why is it effective? In the vast majority of cases you may safely assume that it is a psychological reaction. The victim knows what is being done and, however sophisticated he believes himself to be, however much he laughs at such "nonsense," deep down inside he has the nagging doubt:

". . . but just supposing there *is* something in it . . . !"

Unfortunately for the magic skeptic this explanation does not fit all cases. The victim does not always know what is being done. In the case, above, of the beaten, copper, figure the victim had no idea that the perpetrator even disliked him, let alone hated him to the point of working Black Magic. Certainly the cow did not know it was supposed to run dry! And what about the neighbor's television?

So what makes it work? At present we must be honest and say we do not know. It does not always work. Whether this is because the (would-be) Magician does not truly feel sufficient hatred, again we do not know. Suffice it to say that on many occasions it *does* work and consequently should not be treated lightly. Certainly do not try it "just to see if . . ." Black Magic is dangerous.

V

CEREMONIAL MAGIC

Towards the end of the Middle Ages many of the more learned and moneyed occultists indulged in what is known as Ceremonial Magic, or Ritual Magic. This was an extremely involved process of conjuring up certain spirits and demanding things of them. It involved consecrations and incantations; it needed a great deal of preparation and a certain amount of money; and it seems seldom, if ever, to have worked. Despite these apparent drawbacks Ceremonial Magic has remained popular with the few and is still widely practiced today.

The text-book of the Magician is called a *Grimoire*. The grimoires show how to invoke various infernal powers and how to trick them into, for example, showing where treasure is buried, or giving the Magician the gift of tongues. Many of the more famous old grimoires are still extant. The most famous of these is known as *The Key of Solomon the King*. The oldest known copy of this work, preserved in the British Museum, dates from the sixteenth century. Despite its title it probably originated no earlier than the fourteenth century, and certainly had no real connection with the King of Israel. Other well-known grimoires are *The Sacred Magic of Abra-Melin the Mage, The Grimoire of Honorius, The Black Pullet, The Heptameron, The Lemegaton,* and *The Almadel.* Extracts from these, and other grimoires, will be given in this article. In these magical texts the Magician is exhorted to observe continence and abstinence. He must undress as seldom as possible, sleep little and meditate a great deal. He must fast for a period before the ritual and become pretty much a recluse.

Before dealing with the preparation for the ritual and the ritual itself let us take a look at the variety of spirits available for conjuring. According to the physician to the Duke of Cleves, one Jean Wier, the demons number no less than 7,409,127 together with 79 princes—according to the count he made in the sixteenth century. This figure was "corrected" by Fromenteau, in the same century, to 7,405,920 demons and 72 princes. Since then many others have taken a count and arrived at figures ranging from 666 to 1,758,064,176! However many there actually are, there are certain important ones, leaders of various legions and companies of lesser demons, who are the ones we may attempt to conjure. Each has his own interests; his own field of influence. Working from the *Lemegeton* we find:

AGARES, a Duke from the East. When he makes his appearance it is as a venerable old man riding astride a crocodile. On his wrist perches a hawk. His main purpose is to bring back runaways. He can stop movement itself and can bestow the gift of languages.

AINI is another Duke, but one with three heads. The middle head is a man's but the other two are of a serpent and a cat. He has the body of a well-built man and rides upon a viper. In his hand he carries a blazing torch and enjoys using it to spread destruction. He can teach cunning and knows all things.

AMON is a Marquis. He is very important and has great power. He appears as a wolf with the head of a snake, which breathes fire. He can, however, be made to assume human shape. He can see into the past and the future, and can cause love between enemies.

ANDRAS is another Marquis in the infernal hierarchy. He sports a raven's head on an angel's body. His steed is a wolf, and he carries a mighty sword. Beware should you ever conjure him, for he is dangerous and may kill the Magician himself.

ASMODAY is a powerful King. He, like Aini, has three heads: a ram's, a bull's, and a man's. He rides a dragon and carries a spear. When invoking Asmoday the Magician must be bareheaded. He has many powers, can confer invisibility, teach handicrafts, produce lost treasures, teach math and answer all questions.

BAAL is the King of the East. He may appear as a man or he may change his head for that of a cat or a toad. His voice is hoarse and he gives all varieties of knowledge.

BELETH is another important King. He is extremely reluctant to appear and when he does it is riding on a horse and accompanied by many musicians. He is invariably angry that he has been called and the Magician must use his magical Wand to command him into the right position. Beleth, after all his fuss, is only able to produce love between man and woman.

CIMERIES, again a Marquis, appears dressed as a soldier mounted on a black horse. He teaches grammar and logic, locates buried treasure and is especially knowledgable on matters pertaining to Africa.

DANTALIAN is a powerful Duke. He has many faces, of both men and women, and always carries a book. He teaches the arts and sciences. He knows all human thoughts and can influence men's minds against their will.

FLAUROS appears in the guise of a leopard. He is a Duke and, if commanded, will assume human shape though with fiery eyes and "terrible countenance." He will give truthful answers to all things concerning past, present and future. He is able to destroy the Magician's enemies and keep him from any form of temptation.

FURCAS is another Duke who has the appearance of a cruel old man. He is astride a horse and, like Asmoday, carries a spear. He can teach philosophy, astronomy, and many other sciences.

GAMYGYN arrives in the shape of a horse or a donkey. This Marquis is able to bring the dead back to answer questions. To invoke him, however, necromantic methods are necessary.

GOMORY is a Duke who has the distinction of being the only one to appear in the guise of a beautiful woman. He/She wears a golden crown and can cause the Magician to be loved by all women and girls.

MORAX is both an Earl and President. He appears as a human-headed bull and gives instruction in the liberal sciences, in the magical use of herbs and stones, and in astrology.

MURMUR is both an Earl and Duke. He has a very harsh, rasping voice and rides upon a griffin. He wears his ducal crown and is "announced" by two heralds with trumpets. His main teaching is philosophy and, like Gamygyn, can bring the dead to answer questions.

ORIAS is a powerful Marquis. He appears in the form of a lion riding on a horse. He carries a snake in each hand. He can transform men and bestow dignities. He can also make friends of the Magician's enemies.

PURSON is a King who appears as a big man, but with a lion's head. He carries a viper in one hand and rides on a bear. He will give true answers about the past, present and future and will disclose buried treasure.

SALEOS is a Duke who rides on a crocodile. He is dressed as a soldier, but with his ducal crown. His sphere of influence is to promote love between men and women.

SYTRY, with human body, wings, and the head of any one of a number of wild animals, is classed

41

as a Prince. At the command of the Magician he
will assume fully human form. As well as producing love between men and women he can
make women strip naked before the Magician.
VEPAR, a Duke, assumes the shape of a mermaid. He
is especially connected with the sea. He can cause
storms, death and disaster. He controls the seas
and can cause the delusion of many ships on the
waters.
VINE, a King and Earl, appears as a lion astride a
horse. He, of all the demons, will give the Magician the names of other sorcerers. He can cause
destruction, wreck castles and build defenses. He,
too, can make the waters stormy.
ZAGAN, a King, assumes the shape of a winged bull.
He has the ability to change water into wine, or
into blood, or oil. He can also change any metal
into coin. He can bestow a sense of humor and
is the King of Alchemy.
ZEPAR is a strong Duke, who wears red and is armed
as a soldier. He is the last mentioned in the
Lemegeton. He can inflame women with love for
any men the Magician wishes, and can transform
them into any shape necessary until the men have
enjoyed them.

From this short selection it can be seen that there is
almost certainly a spirit suitable for any possible wish
of the Magician. But having chosen his subject—how to
conjure the appearance? Before anything can be done
the Magician must prepare the tools he will need to use
in the ritual, his vestments, his hat, shoes, the Pentacles,
silken cloth, pen and ink, magic rod, baton, parchment,
water, salt, fire, wax, sword, bell, trident, and most important the Circle itself. The ritual is performed within
an intricate "Magic Circle" which must be accurately
drawn. For if there should be any error in its drawing,
or in the preparation and consecration of any of the

tools, then there will be the loop-hole through which the conjured spirit may leap and seize the Magician.

ROBES

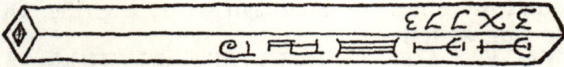

ROD

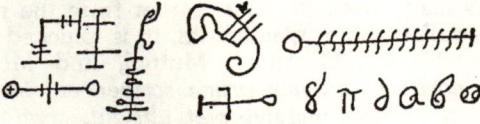

CLOTH

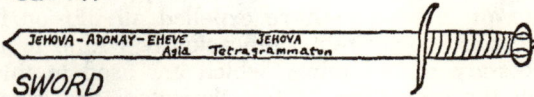

SWORD

TRUMPET

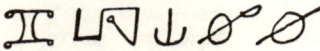

BELL

Fig. 3

In order that the Magician may be pure enough for the ceremony he must spend the nine days leading up to it in meditation and fasting. He must observe complete sexual abstinence. He is allowed only one meal a day—preferably bread and water—and nothing whatsoever on the last day. After each of his meals he must recite:

43

"O grand and powerful and most merciful Adonay, highest of all, I implore thee, in the name of Eloim and Jehowa, to be so pleased as to extend to me thy goodness and guard me in my undertaking. Amen."

His robes must be carefully prepared and consecrated. They are long, flowing garments of purest linen or silk spun, if possible, "by a young virgin." Certain magical characters are to be drawn on the robes with the pen and ink, which have themselves been suitably prepared. Around the robes the Magician wears a girdle, with the following written on it:

"YA, YA, AIE, AAIE—ELIBRA—ELCHIM—SADAI—PAH ADONAI—tuo robore—CINCTUS SUM"

The pen is made from the first feather from the right wing of a swallow or a gander. As it is plucked the Magician must say: "O Angel, Mutuol, and Mumol *Auditorium, nostra et cu hac prima scriber pussim ora experimenta in du nois incipiatur et altsignu creatorum primatur.*" Alternatively he mav say: "Ababaloy, Samoy, Escavor, Adonay, I have expelled all illusion from this pen, that it may retain efficaciously within it the virtue necessary for all things which are used in this Art, as well for operations as for characters and conjurations. Amen."

For the ink there are a number of recipes. "Take peach kernels, put them in a fire, and reduce them to carbon. Take one part of this, mix it with soot, add two parts crushed gall-nut, gum arabic two parts, powder very finely, and sieve all this. This is to be mixed with pure, clean, river water." Or, "Take ten ounces of gall-nut, three ounces of Roman vitriol, some green copperas, rock salt and gum arabic, three ounces of each. Make it all into an impalpable powder but do not make it into ink, but mix when needed." The ink is then consecrated with the following: "I exorcise thee, creature of Ink, by Anston, Cerreton, Stimulator, Adonay, and by the names of Him Whose one Word created all and can achieve all, that so thou shalt assist me in my work, that my work may be accomplished by my will. Amen."

44

The Magician's hat is no more than a crown of virgin parchment with the words "Yod, He, Vau, He" written across the front, with the pen and ink of the Art. His shoes are of white leather. Most important is the Pentacle. This must be made on a Wednesday, at three o'clock in the morning in the first quarter of the moon. Three circles are drawn, one inside the other, on virgin parchment. The outer circle is green, the middle red, and the inner one gold. Within the Circles are written the sacred Names. The Pentacle is then fastened to the Girdle, a blessing is said, and the Pentacle is sprinkled with holy water.

The very important Magic Rod is perhaps the most complicated to prepare. The grimoires stress the precautions pertaining to the secrecy which must be kept regarding it. The Rod should be of virgin hazel wood. That is to say there should be no off-shoots, and it should be no more than a year old. It must be cut in the hour of Mercury, according to the *Key of Solomon*. The *Book of True Black Magic*, however, states that it must be cut in the hour of the Sun. Certain characters are then inscribed on the Rod and the following words said as it is held in the smoke of the incense: *"Adonay, sanctissime et polem, Tetragrammaton, fortisme saday, polentisme adostre et consorate virgula que admode conuent et sanctissime Adonay, regni nosoris fins emna secula secutore. Amen."* ("O Adonay, most Holy and most Powerful, vouchsafe to consecrate and bless this Staff and this Rod, so that it may possess the required virtue, O most Holy Adonay, to whom be honor and glory for ever and ever. Amen.")

The Baton is to be made in the day and hour of Mercury. It is made from walnut wood and has certain signs marked on it. As each of these objects are completed it must be carefully stored away until the time when it will be used. To be stored it must be wrapped in a cloth which, in its turn, has been carefully prepared. The Cloth is of clean, white silk and on it are marked, with the pen and the ink of the Art, yet more sacred signs and symbols. The Sword should be made of unalloyed metal, with a copper or gold handle, and the words *Agla Tetragrammaton* engraved on it. It must be consecrated on a Sunday. The consecration includes being passed through the flames of a fire of laurel and verbena to the words: "O Adonay, great Saint, deign to consecrate this instrument, so that it may be pure. I entreat thee, O Adonay, great Father, who lives and reigns for ever. Amen." It is then wrapped in verbena leaves and placed in the silken cloth. This same consecration is used for the Trident, which is made from hazel wood cut in the light of a full moon. The tree from which it is cut must never have borne fruit, and the blade of the knife that cuts it must never have cut anything previously.

From "black wood" is made the Magic Trumpet. This is blown to the four cardinal points on the Magician's entering the Magic Circle. It must be fumigated in the smoke of the incense and put carefully away until needed, with the other tools. The last important object is the Bell of Invocation. This is a regular hand-bell which has had the letters A V O B Y written inside it, and more signs around its outside.

In the various fumigations it is important that the Magician use the correct incense for the day, and the time of day, that he is working. These are dependent upon the planet which is ruling at the time. For Saturn; use black poppy seed, henbane, myrrh and mandrake. For Jupiter; gum, lignum aloes, the seed of an ash tree. Mars; sulphur, lodestone, gum Armoniack, hellebore. Venus; ambergris, red roses, musk, lignum aloes. Mercury; cloves, cinque-foil, frankincense, mastick. The Sun; ambergris, musk, saffron, frankincense, myrrh. The Moon; white poppy seed, camphor, frankincense.

Next the Water must be consecrated; the Salt and Fire exorcised. Consecration of the Water is effected by reciting the prayer, "Lord, God, powerful and mighty Father, my security, my life, help me. Holy Father, I beseech thee. God of Abraham, God of Isaac, God of

Jacob; God of Angels, Archangels and Prophets, creator of all; I humbly utter this consecration in thy Name, that thou mayest consecrate and bless this water of Great and Holy Adonay, who reigneth without end."

The Salt is exorcised with, "I exorcise thee, creature of Salt, by the Living God, by the God of Gods, and the Lord of Lords that all duplicity go out from thee, and that thou servest us as a strength against all enemies, visible and invisible." The Fire is made in a new iron vessel and is exorcised with, "I exorcise thee, O thou creature of Fire, by Him by Whom all things are made, that forthwith thou cast away every phantasm from thee; that it shall not be able to do any hurt in any thing. Bless, O Lord, this creature of Fire, and sanctify it that no hurt may come to the exorcist or spectators."

Now, at last, the Magician may construct his Magic Circle. The sole purpose of the Circle is to protect the Magician from the evil entities he may conjure up. So long as it is correctly drawn, and he remains within it, no harm can befall him. Great care must therefore be given to this part of the practice.

The main Circle is drawn nine feet in diameter. Within that is drawn a second circle eight feet in diameter. All the holy names of God are then written around in the spaces between the two circles. Outside the Circle, to the North, is drawn a triangle containing a circle, again surrounded by sacred words. This is where the spirit will appear, and from which he may not stray. About the great Circle are drawn pentagrams containing the mighty word *Tetragrammaton*. The Circle should be constructed at the time of the full moon, preferably in the ruins of an old church, castle or monastery. If it must be in an ordinary building then the room should be hung with black curtaining, the doors and windows securely fastened, and only candles utilized for lighting.

With everything now ready the Magician must decide upon the most propitious time to hold his ceremony

The correlation of days and planets, with their governing of matters, is as follows:

Monday:	MOON	—	Theft; merchandise; dreams.
Tuesday:	MARS	—	War; enemies; prison; matrimony.
Wednesday:	MERCURY	—	Debt; fear; loss.
Thursday:	JUPITER	—	Honor; riches; clothing; desires.
Friday:	VENUS	—	Love; friendship; strangers.
Saturday:	SATURN	—	Life; doctrine; building.
Sunday:	SUN	—	Fortune; hope; money.

The hours themselves are governed in the order Sun, Venus, Mercury, Moon, Saturn, Jupiter, Mars; the first hour of each day being the planet of that day (i.e. the first hour of Sunday would be governed by the Sun, of Monday by the Moon, Tuesday Mars, etc. The second hour of Sunday would be Venus, of Monday Saturn, of Tuesday the Sun, etc.

If, then, the Magician is intending to deal with love then he should work in the hour of Venus, or of the Sun; from "the first to the eighth hour, with the Moon in Pisces." Destruction, hate, and the like should be performed on the hour and in the day of Mars; from the first or eighth to the fifteenth or twenty-second hour of the night.

Entering the Circle the Magician lights braziers and burns incense at the four cardinal points. He then passes around, clockwise, within the Circle, saying: "I, who am the servant of the all-highest, do by the virtue of His Holy Name Immanuel, sanctify unto myself the circumference of nine foot about me. From the East GLAURAH; from the West GARRON; from the North CABON; from the South BERITH. Which ground I take for my proper defense from all malignant spirits, that they may have no power over my soul or body, nor come beyond these limitations; but answer truly being summoned, without daring to transgress their bounds. WORRH—WORRAH—HARCOT—GAMBALON."

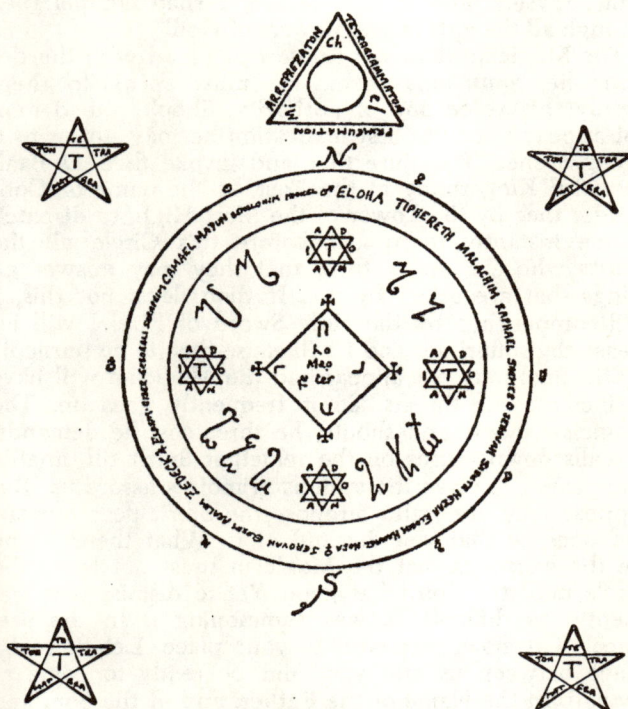

Fig. 4

The Conjuration would now follow and this is determined by the Spirit being summoned. Baal, the King of the East, who gives all knowledge, would be summoned in the following way: "I conjure and I invoke thee, O Baal, strong King of the East, by the names of God, and by my holy work! I order thee to obey me, to come to me, or otherwise to send at once to me Massayel, Ariel, Satiel, Arduel and Acorib, that they may answer my questions, and obey my orders! Now come, thyself: and if thou refuse, I shall compel thee through all the virtues and powers of God!"

The Magician does not *request* or plead with the demons—he *commands* them. He must speak to them sternly; his voice one of authority. Should the demon not appear after the first invocation he may go on to a stronger one: "I conjure thee and invoke thee, O Baal, powerful King ruling at the East, in the name of God! I order thee by the Power of the Most High, to dispatch to me instantly to appear before this Circle all the Spirits who are under thee, that they may answer all things that are asked by me. If thou doest not this, I will compel thee by the Holy Sword of Fire! I will increase thy sufferings, and I will cause thee to be burned!"

Still Baal may not appear and the Magician will have to increase his threats. So it frequently goes on. The Magician shouts and shouts; he threatens, he demands, he calls down curses on the reluctant Spirit till, finally, it appears . . . or so the various grimoires assure us. But suppose they are right. Suppose the Spirit does appear, and does all that you demand of it. What then? Many are the warnings that the Magician must not leave the Circle until the Spirit has gone. Yet to dismiss it is frequently as difficult as was summoning it in the first place! "Go, now, in peace, to your place. Let there be peace between us and you, and be ready to come at my call. In the Name of the Father, and of the Son, and of the Holy Spirit. Amen."

"O Spirit Baal, now that thou hast correctly and diligently completed my tasks and answered my questions, thou mayest leave. Leave, then, without harm to any, man or beast. Leave, then, and be at my disposal whenever I shall call thee again. Leave now, in peace and quiet, I adjure thee! May there be peace between thee and me for ever. Amen."

When the Magician is finally satisfied that the Spirit has departed, then he may leave the Circle. That night, however, should be spent in prayer.

VI

DÉJÀ VU

"I was sitting in the outer office waiting to see the Sales Manager. Suddenly I got this very strong feeling that I had gone through all this before. It was actually my first visit to this particular office yet I knew exactly what was going to happen. The inner door would open and the Sales Manager's secretary would be standing there, a notebook in her hand, looking back into his room. She would laugh at something that was said in there then turn and come out saying, 'Mr. Johnson will see you now, sir.'

"I'd hardly thought of it than it happened. The door opened and there she was, looking back into the room and laughing. The whole little episode went exactly as I knew it would. Every detail; the book in her hand, the color of her dress, her hair-style—everything just as I'd seen it in my mind just a moment before."

The above is a typical example of *déjà vu*—the feeling that you have been somewhere, or done something, before. This is probably one of the most common of "supernatural" experiences and may range from a vague, non-specific, *feeling* to a detailed *knowing*, as in the above example.

A number of possible explanations have been put forward for *déjà vu*. One is that it is proof of reincarnation; that we have literally lived that particular experience before in a previous life and these are vague memories of it. Although that may seem a reasonable explanation when it only involves the feeling of having *been* somewhere before, in the vast majority of cases this is not a sound explanation. If we had lived before the odds against our having been in the exact circumstances with the exact "props" (people, objects) would be astronomical. It would be far more likely that we had been in a very similar situation in this present life and vague memories of that were stirred. Indeed this is the more usual explanation put forward; that some small point reminds our unconscious mind of a previous similar situation and we tell ourselves that all the other points are also remembered. In other words we tell ourselves that we knew what was *going* to happen but in actual fact it was not until it *had* happened that we thought of it as a reoccurrence.

This explanation, then, would be fine if it were not for one thing—there are cases on record where the person has not only known what was going to happen but has actually told a third party what it was. This prior knowing, although labeled *déjà vu* (already seen) should, in the opinion of the author, more correctly be labelled *en avant vu* (seen ahead). For although the usual sensation is that the whole incident has happened before, in the *past*, it would seem far more likely that it is actually a peep into the *future*. It is a precognition, and as such takes on a new interest. *Déjà vu* is accepted as a fairly common occurrence, while precognition seems rare. Now, if *déjà vu* is actually precognition then precognition becomes commonplace. The more complex examples of precognition may now, then, be looked at in a new light—not as singular incidents experienced by a favored few, but as more detailed examples of something experienced at some time by most people.

How can you experiment with *déjà vu?* Unfortunately this is one of the few occasions where you can do nothing to force the issue. You must wait for it to happen. But at least you can be ready for it when it does happen. As soon as you begin to get that feeling "this has all happened before," try hard to think of the details. Exactly *what* has happened before (or, more correctly, is about to happen)? Exactly who will do what? If

53

there is time write down the details. If not at least say them aloud to any other person who might be present. As has been said *déjà vu* is the most common of all experiences, so do not worry that you will be thought of as slightly unbalanced when you suddenly exclaim, "The telephone is going to ring and a girl's voice will ask for Mr. Williams!" As soon as it has actually happened explain the feeling you got. Almost certainly the person to whom you are speaking will admit to having had similar experiences himself.

When you have the feeling of having *been* somewhere before—rather than "re-living" an action, such as a phone call, or an encounter with someone—then recording is easier. For instance, to visit a house for the first time and feel that you have been there before and know it well. Write down, however briefly, descriptions of the various rooms, furniture, ornaments, etc., then go and see if they check out. If they do then you can certainly discount any possibility of fooling yourself *after* seeing, for you will have there the written proof of having known *before* seeing.

VII

DIVINATION

Divination is the method of obtaining knowledge of the unknown or of the future by means of omens. We have elsewhere looked at one or two forms of divination in detail. Here we will deal with other methods not so generally in use.

Alectoromancy was divination by means of a cock. The method is well explained by Jean Baptiste Belot (*Oeuvres*, 1640): "He then who desires to know concerning some matter, whether it be a robbery, a larceny, or the name of a successor, must make upon a very smooth spot a circle which he shall divide into as many parts as there are letters in the alphabet. This done, he shall take grains of wheat and shall place them on each letter, beginning with A and so on continuing, while he says this verse, *Ecce enim veritatem, etc.* The wheat then being thus placed, let him take a young cock or cockerel, perfectly white, and cut its claws; then, having set down this cock, he must take care to watch upon which letters he eats the grains of corn, and, having noted or written these letters upon paper, he must gather them together and then will find the name that he desires to know."

Astragalomancy was the name given to divining by a letter, or symbol, on each of twelve knuckle-bones and then throwing them down on the ground. Variations on this form of casting lots are found all over the world. Australian aboriginals will cast bones of varying lengths; American Indians, such as the Shoshones, will use different shaped stones; Nigerians will use six pieces of wood, each marked with a different design. Depending on how the particular objects fall, so they are interpreted. A modern-day version of casting lots is to use dice. Two of them are used giving twenty-one possible combinations of dice, e.g. 1 and 3; 2 and 5; 4 and 6; etc. There is a list of thirty possible questions that may be asked. The "diviner" selects a question and, thinking hard on it, throws the dice. Each resulting combination has a corresponding thirty answers to the questions. You simply read the answer whose number corresponds to the number of the question asked.

Dream interpretation is known as *Oneiromancy*, and can be one of the most accurate forms of divination. It can also be very revealing about the dreamer, as Freud or Jung would have told you! There are many "dream books" available which aim to explain the hidden meanings of your dreams. For instance, they say that to dream of an altar is a reminder of something unsatisfactory, and may also be associated with the seriousness of the marriage vows. To dream of a barber cutting, or dressing, your hair denotes the ever-present conflict between prestige and success. To dream of a dagger is a threat; a Gypsy, a wish for a change of fortune; an orchestra, means popularity. Such books are really worthless for there can be virtually no generalizations concerning dreams. You can only interpret the altar, or the barber, or the dagger, *in context*. Two different dreams dealing with a dagger could mean two entirely different things.

If you really want to try to explain your dreams, in the sense of divination, then be guided by one of the oldest and most respected "keys" to the occult; namely the Tarot (see separate chapter). Within the seventy-eight cards in the tarot deck you will almost certainly find one which seems closely connected with the dream in question. Interpretation of the symbolism of that card will in turn interpret your dream far better than any of the popular "dream books."

Many people have moles on various parts of their anatomy. If you want to divine by these dark excrescences then you will indulge in *Moleosophy*. Briefly a round mole is an indication of goodness of character; an angular mole of possible badness; and an oblong mole an indication of wealth. Moles on the whole are considered lucky, though lighter colored ones are luckier than darker. The position of the mole on the body is all important and is interpreted thus:

CHEEK: Sombre; studious.
NECK: Good luck; generous.
HIP: Contentment; ingenuity.
ELBOW: Latent talent; urge to travel.
BACK: Cautious; inquiring.
THIGHS: Ill health; sickness.
LEGS: Resourceful; inventive.
CHIN: Generosity; responsible.
BREAST: Laziness; quarrelsome.
ARM: Industrious; happy.
WRIST: Dependable; responsible.
HAND: Wealth; happiness.
BUTTOCKS: Poverty; lack of ambition.
KNEES: Extravagant; amorous.
FEET: Thoughtful; melancholy.

Do you want a method of divination you can work at while sitting on a bus or subway? Why not try *Physiognomy*—character analysis from the face? Again of very ancient origin it can be very interesting, and oftimes amusing, to sit and study the faces around you. One of the first published systems of physiognomy was presented by Johann Lavater, who felt firmly convinced that your face reflected the deepest of your personal traits. Other leaders in this field were Barthélemy Coclès and the Curé Belot.

Classifying by planetary types you will find seven basic faces. The *Solar* type, who has a round, jovial face framed by fair hair. The *Venus* type, who has what might be termed "perfect" features and fair hair. Usually this type has the sweetest smile. The *Martian* type has almost brutal features; rugged, square-cut. The *Mer-*

curial has fine features but dull coloring and black hair. The *Lunar* type is cold, pale and melancholy. The *Jovian* type, noble and bold with strongly marked features. The *Saturnine* type has a mournful look, dark or black hair, and a slightly yellowish complexion.

A face can usually be classed as one of three basic shapes: round, square, or triangular. A round face usually typifies the happy, easy-going type, who enjoys good living and is primarily concerned with achieving a life of ease. He makes friends easily and is a good friend, and loyal. He has every confidence in himself and, so long as he receives the material reward for his work, is quite happy to let others take the credit for it.

The square face is the face of the active, athletic type. He is an all-rounder, making an efficient businessman, but his main enjoyment comes from his out-door activities. Intelligent, yet he will never be a great intellectual. Organizing, yet he will never be the great director. He will plan ahead to an extent, but not too far ahead. He is reliable but not necessarily loyal, for he is not afraid to change his mind. Always interested in anything new, especially anything mechanical.

The triangular face is perhaps the most interesting and certainly the hardest to judge accurately. Usually he has a very quick and active mind; intelligent and analytical. Will not accept anything at its face value but must find out "what makes it tick." He has a great many interests, mostly scholarly. He is not particularly interested in sports. Capable of great concentration, he is excellent at detailed work. You will frequently find that a person born under the Zodiac sign of Virgo has the triangular face. He is inventive and introspective. Inclined to try to follow a number of highly involved projects at one time, he consequently feels frequently frustrated at the limited number of hours in a day. Extreme loyalty is another characteristic.

These three main types of faces may then be modified, one with another, to give the seven planetary types. The traits must then be judged by the balance of the

It is possible to go further and examine the separate features. For instance, a straight nose, in good proportion to the rest of the face, indicates a steady nature, while a large, high-bridged, nose indicates a demanding nature—someone who wants to get things done, and done *his* way. A snub nose, however, indicates an extremely friendly person, perhaps slightly mischievous.

In the same way the eyes, the cheek bones, the ears, the forehead, the chin; all indicate certain properties possessed by the individual. In addition to the actual features, the lines of the face can tell you much. The shapes and angles of the wrinkles when you smile or when you frown, all show deeper, hidden meanings.

Tealeaf reading, or *Tasseography,* is a perennial favorite of the divinity arts. It can be fairly easily learned and will always make you a popular guest at a party! For best results use China tea, brewed in a pot without a strainer, of course. The tea is poured into a cup which should have a wide top and small base. Do not use a cup with any form of pattern on the inside—it could be very confusing!

The subject should drink the tea, but leave sufficient in the bottom of the cup to distribute the leaves around the sides when turned. Ask him to take hold of the han-dle and rotate the cup slowly, three times, clockwise, allowing the tea to come up to the rim of the cup and so be distributed. Then he is to invert the cup com-pletely on its saucer. Taking up the cup from there you can begin your divination. You are going to interpret the various shapes and forms made by the tea leaves on the sides and bottom of the cup. To do this, with some sort of accuracy, there is a time scale you must remember. The rim of the cup, and close to the rim, represents the present and the coming two or three weeks. As you move down the sides so you go further into the future. The very bottom of the cup is the very far distant future. Your starting point is the handle of the cup. This represents your subject, so that symbols that are close to the handle affect him directly while symbols on the opposite side of the cup may only have a passing effect.

If the symbols you see are particularly well defined then they are very lucky. The less well defined, the less decisive and more prone to hindrance. Stars denote success; triangles fortune; squares mean protection; circles represent frustration. Straight lines indicate definite plans; wavy lines, uncertainty; dotted lines mean a journey. Any numbers you may see could be indicators of years, months, weeks, days, or hours. Usually if you see them in the upper half of the cup you can think in terms of hours or days; in the lower half, weeks, months or years. Letters are the initials of people of importance to the subject, be they friends, relatives or business associates.

As with most forms of divination you should interpret what you *feel* about what you see, rather than going by hard and fast "meanings." As a start, however, here are the traditional interpretations of some of the symbols you may see:

ANCHOR: End of a journey. Safe landing. Successful end to a business or personal affair. Problem unexpectedly solved.

ARROW: Disagreement. Antagonism. Instructions for a journey. A letter.

BELL: Good news. Wedding.

BIRD: News, which could be good or bad. Possible journey. Companionship.

BOAT: Travel. End of a friendship.

BOTTLE: Celebration. Success.

BRIDGE: Travel abroad. Partnership. Introduction to new friends or business.

BROOM: End of a problem. Change of jobs. Domesticity.

BUTTERFLY: Insincerity.

CAMEL: Long journey. Temporary re-location.

CAR: Local travel. Introduction to new business associates.

CANDLE: Inovation. Sudden new idea.

CASTLE: Legacy. Unexpected financial luck. Good living.

CAT: Female friend. Domestic problems.

CHAIR: Entertainment. Relaxation.

CHURCH: Marriage. Serious illness (not death).

CLOVER: Good fortune. Unexpected success.

CROSS: Hardship. Discomfort. Misfortune.

CROWN: Honors. Credit. Promotion.

CUP: Love. Close friendship. Harmony.

DAGGER: Danger. Tragedy. Business complications.

DOG: Friendship. Companionship.

ELEPHANT: Advice needed, preferably from an old friend.

FAN: Indiscretion. Disloyalty. Infidelity.

FLAG: Defense necessary. Warning.

FLOWER: Unhappy love affair.

GATE: Opportunity. Possibility of advancement.

GUN: Trouble. Argument. Adultery.

HAMMER: Hard work, which will be rewarded.

HAND: Friendship. Help when needed. Advice.

HARP: Contentment. Ease.

HEART: Love or lover. Confidant.

HORSE: Work.

HORSESHOE: Good luck. Start of a new, successful enterprise.

HOUSE: Security. Authority.

KEY: Opportunity.

KITE: Exercise caution. Think before acting.

KNIFE: Treachery. Duplicity. Misunderstanding.

LADDER: Advancement. Opportunities taken.

MAN: Stranger. Visitor. Help from unexpected source.

MUSHROOM: Disturbance. Complications in business.

PALM TREE: A breathing-space. A rest period. Temporary relief.

PIPE: Thought and concentration needed. Investigate all possibilities.

SCISSORS: Quarrels, usually domestic. Double-dealing.
SNAKE: An enemy. A personal hurt, or an *affaire de coeur*.
TREE: Goal achieved. Comfort. Rest.
UMBRELLA: Temporary shelter.
WHEEL: Advancement through effort. Money.
WINDMILL: Big business dealings.

A form of Tasseography, known as *Geomancy*, can be done using dirt or sand. Mark a circle, about three feet in diameter, on the ground and have the subject throw a handful of dirt into it. You then interpret the symbols made by the dirt in the same way that you did the tea leaves. Similarly, on a smaller scale, draw a circle on a sheet of paper. Blindfold your subject and let him fill the circle with random dots. These dots you may then interpret.

There are many, many more forms of divination that have been used over the ages; divining by the flight of birds, by the marks on the shell of a tortoise, by the course taken by spiders. Many of these have most impressive names. *Libanomancy*, is the art, or science, of divining by the shapes assumed by the smoke rising from burning incense. *Pyromancy* involves studying the rate of burning of various objects thrown on to a fire. *Molybdomancy* is listening to the hisses made when melted lead is allowed to fall into water. *Hydromancy* is the examination of rain water. *Haruspicy* is divining by the inspection of entrails taken from sacrificial animals, or interpreting the cracks that appear in a sheep's shoulder-blade when it is roasted. And so on, with *Aleuromancy, Aeromancy, Axinomancy, Belomancy, Cephalomancy, Cleidomancy, Cromniomancy, Dactylomancy, Daphnomancy, Lampadomancy, Lithomancy, Margaritomancy, Onychomancy, Oinomancy, Oromancy, Sideromancy*, and all the other -mancies. Divination covers a wide area, but any form of it depends on the interpretation of the diviner—on *your* interpretation.

VIII

DIVINING ROD

A divining rod is usually the forked branch of a tree, cut down to convenient size, that a man holds in his hands in a certain manner. Spasmodic movements of the rod will indicate the presence of water, oil, gas, minerals, or virtually anything sought by the operator. When used for finding underground water courses the art is called *rhabdomancy*, "water-witching" or dowsing. The rods are usually cut from the hazel, but all kinds of wood have been used. And not only wood—a frequently used, temporary, rod is made from a bent wire coat-hanger. Although generally discredited by scientists, water-diviners continue to be employed in all parts of this and other countries and, more important, continue to have their successes. One of the best known of present-day diviners in the United States, is Henry Gross, the subject of a number of books on the art.

In his work, *La Phisique occulté ou traite de la baguette divinatoire*, published in 1725, the Abbé de Vallemont describes the rod and its uses: "A forked branch of hazel or filbert must be taken, a foot and a half long, as thick as a finger, and not more than a year old, as far as may be. The two limbs of the fork are held in the two hands, without gripping too tight; the back of the hand being toward the ground. The point goes foremost, and the rod lies horizontally. Then the diviner walks gently over the places where it is believed there is water, minerals, or hidden money. He must not tread roughly . . ." On passing over the spot where the water, metal, or whatever, lies hidden the branch will twist in the operator's hands until it is pointing down at the source. The twist can be so violent that it breaks the branch.

One successful diviner described how he found water, by saying, "I just cut a green fork off a peach tree—some use witch hazel or redbud, but peach always works for me—and take one prong in each hand. Then I walk slowly back and forth, holding the fork in front of me, parallel with the ground. When I cross an underground stream the stick turns in my hands, so that the main stem points toward the water. Then I drive a stake in the ground to mark the place, and that's where I tell 'em to dig their well." Asked how he judged the depth you would need to dig to get to the water he said, "Well, I judge by the strength of the pull on the stick. If the water's too far down it doesn't register at all, and the nearer it is to the surface, the stronger it pulls. I just kind of guess at it."

Guessing may be all very well but it is possible to find the depth exactly. Another diviner holds the stick up, after its initial twist down, and literally asks it "How far down?" He then starts counting. "Ten feet, twenty feet, thirty feet . . ." The stick twists again, hard, at the appropriate depth. Some diviners claim that they must be "insulated from the ground" to operate properly. They insist they can only work wearing rubber soled and heeled shoes. It has been found that these diviners work just as well when they only *think* they are wearing their rubber-bottomed shoes. They may wear composition soles or the like and, believing them to be rubber, have their usual successes.

If divining for other than water then it is as well to fasten a "witness" to the rod. This is a sample of what you are seeking. If you are divining for gold, then slip a gold ring over the end of the rod; if for silver, fasten a silver dollar to it. You can have a lot of fun, and useful practice, by "planting" a source. It can also save an awful lot of digging! Have a friend bury a half-dollar. It can either be actually buried in the ground or it can be placed under a flat stone. Then take your divining-rod. Try various types of wood. It should be shaped like a large sling-shot, the branches about eighteen inches long and an inch thick. Hold it firmly near the ends of the two branches, the backs of the hands towards the ground and the thumbs outwards. Have the point of the rod pointing either straight ahead or up at an angle of roughly forty-five degrees. Scotch-tape another half dollar to the pointing end of the rod. Now you are ready to go.

Walk slowly but firmly, your arms held out in front away from the body. Walk systematically to cover the whole area of ground. Do not be disappointed if you cannot locate the half dollar on your first try—or even your first dozen tries. Just be thankful that you are not having to dig down twenty or thirty feet each time before you find you are wrong! When you do get response, at the proper spot, you will find that the rod will twist over and down of its own volition. Nothing you can do will stop it. If you grip really hard you may succeed in stripping the bark from the twisting wood, but stop it you will not.

A variation, particularly if you lack clear, open, ground, is to fasten a photograph to the rod and have the subject of the photograph hide behind a bush or tree. The divining can even be turned into a party game by blindfolding the diviner and laying a coin on the rug, or behind a cushion.

Whatever you use, wherever you do it, keep records of your hits, your misses, and your "close proximities." Try different woods. Experiment. You may find you have an especial gift for divining. Even if the United States Geological Service of the Department of the Interior thinks diviners are fakes, there are many thousands of people who do not. And there are many, many people, each year, who make use of diviners. People like farmers, gas and electric companies, municipal water and sewage companies. If you do find that you have the gift, get in touch with the American Society of Dowsers, Rhode Island. They will be happy to hear from you.

IX

ECTOPLASM

In the world of Spiritualism are found two main types of mediums; mental and physical. The physical medium is the one who produces phenomena observable by the sitters, the audience, themselves. Of the knocks, lights, moving objects, and other phenomena produced by these mediums the most tantalizing is ectoplasm. From a distance ectoplasm looks a lot like a piece of damp cheese-cloth which molds itself into shapes representing persons long since dead. Mediums who produce ectoplasm, and there seem to be fewer and fewer of them as the years go by, usually work in darkened, or semi-darkened, rooms. The ectoplasm itself is slightly luminous. The reason for this darkness, they say, is that light destroys ectoplasm or, at worst, makes it extremely difficult to produce.

In *A Dictionary of Modern Spiritualism*, Norman Blunsdon describes the substance as "a subtle living matter present in the physical body, primarily invisible but capable of assuming vaporous, liquid, or solid states and properties . . . it possesses a characteristic smell and is cold to the touch." This "subtle living matter" exudes from the various orifices of the medium's body and afterwards returns thence. When not molding itself into quasi-human bodies it acts as a "rod" to support a trumpet, through which a voice may speak, or to levitate a table or other object.

There have been infra-red photographs taken of mediums producing ectoplasm and, in all fairness, it must be said that some of the pictures are startling and extremely convincing. In *The Supernatural* (Hawthorn Books, New York, 1965) Hill and Williams include some excellent photographs of British medium Jack Webber producing ectoplasm. Not quite so convincing are the photographs taken at a spiritualist summer camp in Pennsylvania, where the purported manifestation of the medium's guide looks remarkably like someone with a piece of painted cheese-cloth thrown over his head. This, however, may be the nature of the beast. Not having seen actual ectoplasm myself I cannot say. It is regrettable, certainly, that more physical mediums are not available, or willing to be investigated, that more may be found out about this strange substance.

If ever you should hear of such a medium, and should be able to arrange a sitting, do not hesitate to do so. If you can arrange to take infra-red photographs then do so, and advise such a body as the American Society for Psychical Research, or the Parapsychology Foundation, of the outcome. If you cannot take photographs then sketch or make detailed notes. Try not to be too skeptical, nor be too gullible. Observe and record—there is plenty of time to make up your mind later.

X

EXTRA-SENSORY PERCEPTION (ESP)

Extra-sensory perception, or *psi*, is today accepted as fact. Thanks for this are chiefly due to Dr. J. B. Rhine and Dr. S. G. Soal, two pioneer experimenters in this field. Serious investigation of possible "thought transference" dates from the late nineteenth century when a number of experiments were conducted, with different subjects, by Mrs. A. Verrall and C. P. Sanger, in England. By the late nineteen-twenties, in similar experiments, Miss I. Jephson and R. A. Fisher had found that every-day playing cards were not the ideal instruments for testing purposes, since persons tend to favor certain cards over others. This led to the introduction of the Zener deck of cards: twenty-five cards—five each of five different designs. The designs are very simple, basic ones: circle, square, cross, wavy lines, and star. Today these cards are used almost exclusively in ESP experiments.

Very simply the point of ESP testing is to find whether or not one person can "guess" what is in another person's mind a greater number of times than would be expected by chance. With the one person looking at the twenty-five Zener cards it is known that the second person would guess correctly which card was being looked at only five times out of the twenty-five if it were left purely to chance. Going through the deck a number of times, then, the *average* right guesses would be five per twenty-five cards. As an example of what has been achieved in such tests, a Mr. Hubert E. Pearce, Jr., when being tested at Duke University, Durham, N.C., guessed correctly 3,746 cards out of 10,300. More recently in London, B. Shackleton guessed right 1,101 cards out of 3,789—this time guessing not the actual card being looked at, but the card that was going to be looked at next! Such scores, carried out under laboratory conditions, prove beyond doubt that extra-sensory perception is a fact.

Just what is meant by "laboratory conditions?" If two people sit down facing one another, at opposite sides of a room, and one holds the cards in front of him while the other tries to guess the card, no matter how impressive the score it cannot be considered seriously. These are *not* laboratory conditions, in that many minor factors may have contributed to help the Guesser. The cards may have had odd marks, spots, specks, clues of some sort on their backs that would help the Guesser, unconsciously perhaps, differentiate one card from another. The face of the Sender might have been another factor—an unconscious facial movement; even a slight murmuring from the lips. No, for the results to be seriously considered many precautions must be taken. Firstly the two participants must *not* be in the same room; moving on from one card to the next would be signaled by a flashing light or a buzzer. Even the cards would not be picked by the Sender; they would be shuffled by a machine and put into truly random order. Every possible precaution would be taken—and even then, if your mind is set against it, you could discount the results! For if a person guesses, say, 8,000 cards correctly out of 10,000 (astronomical odds against chance), who is to say that if he went on to try another 10,000 he might not be so far out that his over-all score would be brought down to "average," or below? Just where does one draw the line? Without going to such lengths, however, there are a number of experiments which you can do to test for extra-sensory perception. For these experiments you may use Zener cards, regular playing cards, or just plain paper and' pencil, as will be seen.

In the laboratory the two experimenters are termed the *agent* and the *percipient*. We will call them simply the *Sender* and the *Receiver*. (The author feels that the person concentrating at the card is as important as the person trying to guess it.)

Let us start with the two experimenters in the same room. Later on we will elaborate on this set-up. Now although they are in the same room we will put them at opposite sides of the room, and with their backs to one another. We might also erect some sort of screen between them in the center of the room. Even a curtain will do. In addition to the Sender and Receiver we will need a Supervisor and, of course, a Note-taker. Records of the proceedings are all important in any aspect of parapsychology, but especially so in checking for ESP. The Supervisor could also take the notes if there is no one else to do so but it is much better if he is free to direct the proceedings.

The Sender has a deck of Zener cards, which has first been well shuffled by the Supervisor, and the resulting order noted on a sheet of paper and placed in his pocket. In front of the Receiver is a picture of each of the five Zener designs; star, wavy lines, circle, square, cross.

The Supervisor gives the word "Start," and the Sender turns up the top card on the deck and thinks hard on the design. The Receiver then *points* (no word is to be spoken by either Sender or Receiver) to the design he feels is the one on which the Sender is concentrating. The Note-taker records the design and signals the Supervisor to call for the next card. (An alternate method, without a Note-taker, is for the Receiver to write down his guesses rather than just pointing.) And so they go through the twenty-five cards. The Supervisor will then re-shuffle them, note their order, and pass them back to the Sender to be gone through again.

Go through the deck a number of times before checking on how the score is going. The fact that the record of the cards' order is kept in the pocket of the Supervisor ensures that the Receiver is not "picking up" from anyone other than the Sender. The Note-taker's job is solely to record the guesses and signal when the next card is required.

Checking the score for one run through we might find something like this:

CARD	GUESS
square	square
wavy lines	star
circle	cross
circle	wavy lines
cross	circle
square	star
star	star
wavy lines	cross
star	square
square	wavy lines
star	star
circle	circle
square	circle
cross	square
circle	cross
wavy lines	wavy lines
star	square
circle	circle
cross	cross
cross	wavy lines
wavy lines	star
square	square
star	circle
wavy lines	cross
cross	wavy lines

A total of eight correct guesses out of twenty-five. Although above what would be expected by chance, do not get excited yet! The next run-through might produce only three correct out of twenty-five. This is why we must do a number of runs-through. The more we do, the truer picture we will get.

But let us suppose that on checking we find a typical result looks like the table on page 73.

This gives a total of only three correct guesses out of twenty-five. On the face of it not very impressive. But look at the results again. The second card looked at was the wavy lines. The Receiver incorrectly guessed a circle. But when the next card, a cross, was studied the Receiver came up with the wavy lines—*the guess was one card behind*. Similarly the sixth card was a square against the seventh guess of a square; the seventh card a star against the eighth guess of a star. *Each guess was one card behind*. Looking at the full run again then, and comparing the "second guesses" to the cards, we find a score of twelve correct out of twenty-five. Very much more interesting. In the same way it may have been found that, like Mr. B. Shackleton mentioned earlier, the Receiver is guessing one *ahead* of the Sender. Or it could be two ahead; or even in reverse order! Again, though, these results cannot be looked at by themselves but must be taken as part of a series.

We can now start to elaborate a little, and approach more towards the "laboratory conditions." Have the Sender and Receiver in separate rooms. It will now be necessary to arrange some indicator to signal when it is time to move on to the next card. The Note-taker, in the room with the Receiver, could shout to the Supervisor but that is hardly the best method. It should be fairly easy to arrange a light that could be flashed, using a flashlight battery and bulb and a length of wire.

The next step would be to separate the two experimenters by an even greater distance, and this actually can be a very easy operation. The Sender is in one house, with the Supervisor; the Receiver is in another

CARD	GUESS
square	wavy lines
wavy lines	circle
cross	wavy lines
circle	cross
circle	star
square	circle
star	square
wavy lines	star
star	wavy lines
square	cross
star	square
circle	square
square	circle
cross	star
circle	cross
wavy lines	circle
star	wavy lines
circle	cross
cross	star
cross	cross
wavy lines	wavy lines
square	square
star	square
wavy lines	star
cross	circle

house, with the Note-taker. The houses may be across the street from each other; opposite sides of town; even several towns apart. At a pre-arranged time, when all is ready, the Supervisor will telephone the Note-taker and, with Supervisor and Note-taker remaining on the phone to each other, continue as if they were all in the same room.

A further, and often significant, aspect of the Receiver's guesses is how strongly they are felt. For this reason it is a good idea to note whether he receives the impression strongly or weakly. If he gets the "chance" score of five out of twenty-five it would be a far greater indication of possible ESP to find that each of the five hits had been very definite impressions to the Receiver, than if he had just felt that "possibly" they were right. Guesses, then, might be recorded as STRONG and WEAK (e.g. "1—circle; weak. 2—star; weak. 3—star; strong. 4—cross; weak. 5—square; strong." etc.)

If you do not have the Zener cards then there is no reason why you should not start off using regular playing cards. In fact there are many ways of testing that can make the whole thing that much more interesting. If you have a deck of Tarot cards (q.v.) try using them. With seventy-eight cards in the deck you would not need to go through them so many times as with the Zener cards. Other possibilities are numbers—perhaps using dominoes; words—with a dictionary opened at random. For these it would really be necessary for the Receiver to write down the guesses himself or tell them to the Note-taker, thus ruling out the same-room set up. Yet another method is for the Supervisor to go through a number of newspapers and magazines and clip out simple illustrations. The Receiver is then armed with pencil and pad and has to sketch the pictures being studied by the Sender.

If there are a number of people in a group who are interested in ESP there is no reason why the above experiments should not be carried out using two small groups. One group, as Senders, would concentrate on the card, number, word or picture, while the other group, as Receivers, record their individual impressions. Later the positions could be reversed; the first group would act as Receivers and the second as Senders.

While you must not be too quick to jump to the conclusion that there is definitely ESP between any two particular people, at the same time do not go to the other extreme. Do not say—as mentioned earlier—that if you keep on long enough the scores can only even out to chance. For instance, many married couples find that, after some years of living together, they frequently think or say the same thing at the same time. Parapsychologists invariably shrug this off by saying that over the years the two just tend to think along the same lines —a chain of thought may be triggered which follows the same course in each of them. Although this is probably very sound reasoning, let us not close our eyes entirely to the possibility that ESP might well play a frequent part in such "similar thinkings." So little is really known of the hows, whys and wherefores of extra-sensory perception that no one can say definitely that it is not a power which may develop and strengthen between two people over a period of time.

XI

HAUNTINGS

Have you ever seen a ghost? (Actually *apparition* is the preferred term these days.) Have you *heard* a ghost (for some will not reveal themselves)? Have you ever encountered a poltergeist? If you did experience any of these things what was the first thing you did? I hope it was to make a very careful note of everything you thought you saw or heard?

In 1901 two Englishwomen, Miss Jourdain and Miss Moberley, were on a visit to Versailles. At the Petit Trianon they suddenly found themselves walking through scenes from the eighteenth century. They saw, or so they believed, such people as Marie Antoinette and members of Louis XVI's court. Unfortunately what might have been one of the most grandiose ghost scenes in history is now held as insignificant because the two ladies did not bother to put down on paper what they experienced until nine years afterwards.

Obviously human memory can play all kinds of tricks over that period of time. To wait *one* year would have been too long. So if you have any type of haunting experience at all, write it down straight away. It does not matter *how* you write it—style, punctuation, grammar, are unimportant. Just get it down while it's fresh.

The word APPARITION comes from the Latin *appare*, to appear. A ghost is the apparition, or appearance, of someone (or some animal) deceased. Not all apparitions are visual; they may be auditory, tactile, or even odoriferous. Not all apparitions are unfriendly. Many are friendly to the point where families, living in the house haunted by the apparition, would feel distinctly sad if "their ghost" went away. What causes an apparition? It is invariably connected with some traumatic experience, or a violent death—perhaps murder. Let us look at a few typical hauntings.

In 1963 Ed and Sena Szurszenski bought a house in Hawthorne Street, Pittsburgh. The house had been on the market for over a year despite the popularity of the neighborhood. They had not been in their house long before they began to realize that unusual things were happening. By habit both husband and wife were extremely tidy. They would never leave closet doors open, for instance. Yet time and again the door to a closet in the kitchen and the door to the bathroom medicine cabinet would be found wide open. Ed Szurszenski took the trouble to check the doors for balance, and to check their catches. All was fine.

Floors would creak in the early morning as they did only when someone walked on them. The house seemed to become more and more depressing.

Finally, one day, Sena heard someone sob. She had learned that the husband of the house's former owner had committed suicide in the garage. Feeling that he might well be the "ghost" Sena called him by name. She was startled to receive an answer. By interrogating this disembodied voice she learned that he had not killed himself at all. His death had been accidental, and he wanted his family to know this.

The proof came later, as the voice told her it would. When installing a new furnace they came across a dried-up bottle of insulin in the cold air return. Presenting it to the voice Sena was told that, unknown to his wife and two daughters, he had suffered from diabetes. Leaving for work one morning the bottle had fallen from his coat and rolled into the cold air return. As he waited for his car to warm up he suffered an attack and, while in a coma, the garage door had slid down. When his wife came downstairs nearly an hour later it was too late.

It was not until Sena and Ed Szurszenski had given

the whole story to the widow that they learned the significance of the swinging doors. It had been the habit of the late husband to read a poem taped to the inside of each door every morning. Once the news that her husband had not committed suicide had been imparted to the former owner, Sena and Ed heard no more from their invisible companion.

In 1810, John Chave and his family lived in the little village of Sampford Reverell, Devon, England. One day the family and servants were startled to hear bangs and thumps in practically every room in the house. John Chave himself, getting over his first shock, experimented and found that if he stamped on the floor, or thumped the walls, similar bangs and thumps would "answer" him from other rooms. If he were downstairs the answers would come from upstairs, and vice versa.

This in itself was not unbearable but it soon became impossible for anyone to sleep in the house. A large, iron, candlestick would move about a room; a sword, placed with a Bible on the foot of one of the beds, was thrown vigorously across the room; Ann Mills, a servant, was beaten across the back as she went to strike a light; objects were wrested out of people's hands and then thrown about. Curtains were moved about; women were beaten; the house shook.

The Rev. C. C. Colton, of the village, investigated the activities, as did many others, and was unable to offer any explanation. He closed all windows and doors and put his personal seal on them. He interviewed all the servants and family members. He arranged for other people to stay in the house and note their findings. Finally, exhausting all possible explanations, he offered one hundred pounds (about $1500 today) reward to anyone who could discover the cause of the disturbances. The phenomena continued for over three years till finally the house was left empty. A satisfactory explanation of the case has never been found.

Two Lieutenants of the Royal Flying Corps chatted together in the room of one of them, Lieutenant Larkin, on the morning of December 17th, 1918. Lieutenant Connell, Larkin's visitor and close friend, then left to fly a plane to Tadcaster and back. They promised to meet on his return, which would be late that afternoon.

It was only early afternoon when the door to Larkin's room opened and, looking up, he saw Lieutenant Connell standing there. There was no mistaking him, for the light was good and he was only a few feet away. Larkin was surprised to see him back so soon and said so. Connell replied that he had made a particularly good trip and would see his friend in the mess-room. He then went out and closed the door.

When Larkin went to the mess-room, later, he was surprised to find no sign of Connell. It was not until evening that he learned that Lieutenant Connell had been killed when his plane crashed near Tadcaster early that afternoon.

Here we have had three typical hauntings. Each has, incidentally, been investigated and authenticated. The first was an auditory ghost though also able, apparently, to open closet doors and cause floors to squeak when he walked on them. The second was very much the poltergeist (literally, *rattling ghost*), throwing things about and making a terrific noise. (This particular poltergeist seems to have differed a little from the "usual" in that it actually harmed people. Most poltergeists, for all their noise and their damage to property, would not actually harm you.) Lastly there was a very definite apparition. The appearance of a person, to all intents and purposes flesh and blood, who had actually been killed many miles away, possibly at the very moment of his appearance. The visual apparition does not always have this flesh and blood look. Quite often the viewer realizes that he can see through the apparition, or even walk through it.

The usual thing, on encountering a ghost or a haunted

house, used to be to call a priest and have him exorcise it. Unfortunately this did not always do the trick, especially if the ghost, in his material life, had not been particularly religious. These days people are more inclined to contact a psychic researcher—and this is where *you* come in. Britain has for years had many amateur and professional Ghost Hunters. With the increasing interest in the whole field of the paranormal in America we may soon have a Ghost Club similar to the British one, where groups go out to investigate using every possible device for detection.

But apart from any scientific instruments there are certain qualifications you will need. First and foremost are powers of observation. Apparitions usually occur unexpectedly and may last fleetingly. You must note every possible detail while you can. Is it transparent or does it appear solid? Does it walk normally or does it seem to glide? Is it three-dimensional or "flat?" Every little detail must be taken in.

You must be in good health. Frequently you will be sitting up all night, usually in an uncomfortable position, just waiting, watching and listening. Your hearing, of course, must be good, as must your eyesight. You must possess tact and diplomacy for often you will see or hear nothing yourself but must interview a person who has.

It will help tremendously if you have even a rudimentary knowledge of conjuring and sleight of hand—this especially in poltergeist occurrences. For a large number of supposed poltergeist occurrences have been traced to a mischievous child in the family, or even to an adult hungry for publicity.

Suppose you hear of a haunted house and get permission to investigate. How will you set about it? First you will interview everyone who has seen or heard the ghost. Get every possible detail you can. If the ghost has been seen on a number of occasions find out if it is always in the same place. Does it follow a definite route? This is important for setting up your equipment. If the ghost always appears at the top of the stairs, glides silently down them and out the front door, then there will be little point in you keeping watch in the kitchen. This may sound obvious but it is amazing how often an over-enthusiastic amateur ghost-hunter can go running off without planning ahead, and miss the whole thing.

Set a series of lengths of thread across the stairway, the hallway and the front door. If they are broken after the "ghost's" passage—it was a very earthy ghost! Try to position yourself midway along the route. Have a tape-recorder to record any possible sounds made. You will need a camera—preferably two. Position the camera(s) at the spot from which the ghost was previously seen. It is frequently said that ghosts cannot be photographed yet once in a while a seemingly authentic picture does turn up. One of your cameras should be loaded, if at all possible, with infra-red film—the other with regular, though fast speed film. If your second camera could be a movie camera all the better. Another very useful piece of equipment is a thermometer—a regular maximum-minimum one will do. Supposedly there is a very definite drop in temperature during the occurrence of supernatural phenomena.

What can be done if the ghost is non-visual? Or if it is visual but just does not put in an appearance when you are there? If it is auditory then obviously you will use your tape-recorder. But there are other things you can do. Hold a séance, for instance. Take along your Ouija board, or set up your own as described in the chapter on talking boards, and try to contact the ghost that way. An alternative is automatic writing. The most interesting way, however, and the one most likely to produce results, is by hypnosis. Take along someone who is a good hypnotic subject and seat him (or her) in the room or passageway especially associated with the ghost. He should be told nothing of any known details concerning the haunting. No discussion of the happenings should be held in his presence prior to the hypnotic session at the site.

When the subject is comfortably seated trance should be induced. The deeper the trance the better. If the subject can be taken to the somnambulistic stage then he should be told that there is a spirit present who would like to make use of his voice. It will only be for a short time and he is to let the spirit take over. You will pause for a moment and then ask, as with the Ouija board, "Is there anybody there?" Invariably you will get a reply from, and then be able to question, the spirit responsible for the haunting.

Here again your tack and diplomacy will come in. You may well have to quiet an angry spirit or console a depressed one. It could even be that the ghost is unaware of the fact that he is "dead." This is not uncommon and is, indeed, the very reason for his clinging to the scene of his lifetime. In such a case your job is to bring to the ghost realization of his state and convince him to move on along his allotted path, leaving the house to its present occupants.

At the end of the "interview" bid the spirit farewell and, with a brisk change of tone, call your hypnotic subject by name and tell him to return to the control of his own voice. Then bring him out of the trance. There need be no fear of the spirit refusing to leave, for it is only the use of the vocal chords which it has had. It has not taken over the entire body. The act of bringing the subject out of the trance will always ensure the disengagement of the spirit.

If it is only possible to put your hypnotic subject into the lethargic or cataleptic stages then it is still possible to question the ghost. You would ask the questions and the subject would relay the replies, rather than having them come direct.

e.g.   HYPNOTIST: "What is your name?"
      SUBJECT: "He says his name is John . . . John Hudson."

Throughout such an interview you would run a tape-recorder and, if possible, take shorthand notes. The interesting part comes after the séance, be it Ouija board, automatic writing, or hypnosis—that is, the checking of the information received. This is the most essential part of the investigation and one on which even professional investigators have fallen down. *Always* check your results. If they are not substantiated by known facts then they should be disgarded and a further séance planned.

One final word on ghosts, or apparitions. I said that they are appearances of people or animals *deceased*. Some people, I know, would take issue on this and point to cases of an apparition appearing in one place while the person was still alive—if only just—in another. I would class *such* appearances as Astral Projections. The line between the two is fine indeed. In fact ghosts are no more than Astral bodies finally separated from their physical bodies. But that is where I draw the line —if the physical body *is* still alive, it is not a ghost but a projection.

XII

HYPNOSIS

Many years after Franz Anton Mesmer's "cures" had rocked the world, when talk of universal fluids, animal magnetism, and the like had died down, James Braid investigated the phenomena and decided that it was not all fraud. Reappraising the various theories this English surgeon, in the mid-nineteenth century, finally decided that there was a definite science, a science of sleep, which he termed *hypnotism*. For his pains poor Braid was discredited in his own country, and barred from practicing medicine, by the extremely conservative medical authorities of his day. His work had, however, attracted attention and people like Charcot, in France, took up his ideas and expanded them.

Despite connotations of evil and danger linked with hypnotism over the years, by the more sensational novelists, it gradually struggled out of the realms of magic into the realms of science. From the "sleep temples" of ancient Greece to the dental chairs, among others, of present-day America hypnosis today has become a major medical tool and, as you will see, an important tool in psychic research. Hence its inclusion in a book of this type, dealing with the supernatural.

But who can hypnotize and who can be hypnotized? Is it a gift given to the few? Certainly not. Almost everyone can learn to hypnotize. It is simply a case of study and practice. Unfortunately the reverse is not true—not everybody can be hypnotized, though certainly a large percentage can. To destroy one fallacy, the subject does *not* have to be weak-willed in order to be hypnotized—in fact quite the reverse. A strong-willed person, with good intelligence and *wanting* to be hypnotized, is probably. the best subject. I stress the fact that the subject must *want* to be hypnotized for it is very difficult indeed to hypnotize a person against his will.

There are a number of simple tests which you can give to find the susceptibility of potential subjects. They are aimed at testing to what degree a person is able to relax. I list a few here which may be tried with individuals or with a group of people. You may well think of others yourself.

1. Ask your subjects if they have ever tried to relax completely; relaxing the entire body? Or have they ever tried to relax completely just one single part of the body; an arm, for instance? Ask them to join in a simple experiment to see just how completely they can relax an arm. They are to sit up straight, their feet flat on the floor—no legs crossed. Each one is then to bend up one arm, say the right, and extend the forefinger. On this raised finger each is to rest the left hand. The whole of the left hand and arm is then to be completely relaxed, so that it is only the right arm which holds it up. When they have done this explain that you will count to three and on the "three" they are to rapidly remove the supporting right hand. If they have truly relaxed the left arm it should immediately fall in their lap. Count, then, your "one, two, *three!*" As the right hands are withdrawn the arms will come down at varying speeds. Those whose arms fall most easily are the ones in whom you are interested as potential hypnotic subjects.

2. Explain again that here is a simple experiment to test how completely a person can relax. Have a subject stand a little in front of you, with his feet together, arms at his sides, and with his back to you. Point out to him a spot on the ceiling at, roughly, a forty-five degree angle, and have him gaze on it. Then start to tell him how relaxed he is: "Relax, now. Relax completely.

Your arms are loose at your sides; you are completely at ease. Don't be afraid if you should feel you are falling back.. I won't let you fall. Just relax, completely at ease."

If you continue like this for a while the subject will very soon sway backwards and fall into your arms—and do be ready for it! If he should not start to fall then reach forward and pull very, very gently on his shoulder. The person who falls back easily is the more susceptible to hypnosis; the person who strains to remain upright is too tense.

3. As with the previous test have the subject stand, feet together, slightly ahead but this time facing you. With your arms raised your fingertips should just touch his temples. Have him look into your eyes and again give the suggestions of complete relaxation, speaking this time of falling forwards. As you speak you can exert the very slightest pressure on the temples to draw him towards you. Again, if he falls forwards easily, obviously relaxed, he should be a good subject.

After trying these three experiments, in the order given, pass on to one or two based more directly on susceptibility to suggestion rather than initial relaxation. Ask your subjects to clasp their hands together, intertwining the fingers. They are then to raise their clasped -hands up into the air, above their heads. Tell them, then, to turn over the hands, keeping them together, so that the palms are uppermost. Then lower them on to the tops of their heads, and press the two hands together. Next tell them that you will count to three, and at "three" they are to try to pull their hands apart, but— *they will not be able to separate them!* Then count, "one, two, *three!*" A number of people will have no problem separating their hands, but quite a few will have great difficulty—some even finding it impossible. These are the people who will make good subjects. When you have made a mental note of who they are, tell them to stop trying to separate their hands, and relax. They are then to turn their hands right way up and bring them down to their laps where they will separate quite easily.

Having selected your subject you can now prepare to hypnotize. Remember, here, that your surroundings are all important. Forget the theatrical hypnotist who seems able to put anyone to sleep right there on the stage. His technique, a type of "shock" hypnosis, has no place here. You want a room where you can be quiet and free from interruption. Late afternoon or evening are the best times. The subject may either sit in a chair or lie on a couch, the aim being that he should be completely comfortable and able to relax fully. You should explain to him that there is nothing whatever to fear, that when he wakes he will probably feel better than he has in a long time. You yourself must exude confidence. Do not take the attitude, "Let me see if I can hypnotize you." Rather give the impression that this is just one more in a long line of successful experiments.

There are three stages, or levels, of hypnosis, for all practical purposes. The *Lethargic* stage, the *Cataleptic* stage, and the *Somnambulistic* stage. The first of these is the lightest. The subject can hear all that is being said. His eyes are closed and he does all that is asked of him, yet he does not believe he is hypnotized. He feels that he could actually open his eyes and sit up any time, if he wished—but he just cannot be bothered. He feels the hypnotism did not really work, but he is willing to go along with it. When awakened he can remember all that ensued.

The cataleptic stage is a little deeper. The subject does all he is asked to do but does not necessarily feel he can wake himself up at any point. His limbs feel especially heavy, and if he is told he cannot bend an arm he will find that he really cannot bend it. When awakened he can remember a little of what happened but not all .

. The somnambulistic is the deepest stage. The subject

remains completely passive. He makes no moves whatsoever without being instructed to do so. He will answer questions and do all that is asked of him, yet will have no memory of it on -awakening. Some subjects will go easily into the somnambulistic stage. For others to get there takes many sessions.

There are various techniques of hypnosis but the basis of all of them is a tiring, or straining, of the eyes, together with suggestions of sleep. The eyes, feeling strained, will close and this along with the verbal suggestions, will bring sleep, albeit hypnoidal. While the suggestions remain much the same the methods of tiring the eyes differ. One method is to have the subject gaze into your own eyes. Stand in front of your seated subject, with your face about fifteen inches in front of, and a foot or so above, the level of his eyes. His back should be directly under the source of light. Tell him to keep looking into your eyes, trying to think of nothing in particular. Then start on your induction:

"Relax . . . relax and breathe deeply . . . keep looking into my eyes and relax . . . relax every muscle in your body . . . breathe slowly and deeply. Concentrate on my voice . . . presently you will notice a very pleasant feeling of heaviness coming over your entire body. Relax . . . you are warm and comfortable . . . you are at ease. Relax and think of sleep . . . . . . breathe deeply . . . evenly. You can feel your whole body relaxing . . . you can feel your legs going to sleep. Breathe deeply . . . everything is fine. You are at ease . . . your legs are asleep . . . your hands and your arms are going to sleep . . . sleep . . . relax . . . your body is asleep. You want to sleep . . . you are fine . . . you are comfortable . . . your eyes feel tired . . . your eyelids feel heavy. Breathe deeply . . . you are at rest . . . you want to sleep . . . your eyelids want to close. You want to sleep . . . to sleep . . . your eyelids are so heavy . . . they want to close. Your eyes are becoming very watery and heavy. They are beginning to flutter . . . you can hardly keep your

88

eyes open. Breathe deeply . . . relax . . . allow your mind to become very passive . . . you just want to close your eyes and fall fast asleep . . . sleep . . . sleep . . . the moment you close your eyes you will fall into a deep, sound, hypnotic, sleep . . . you will continue to listen to my voice . . . I will count to three. When I reach three you will find it impossible to keep your eyes open . . . you will close them and sleep . . . a deep, deep, hypnotic, sleep . . . relax . . . relax . . . one . . . breathe deeply . . . two . . . relax . . . you're fine. You're comfortable . . . three. Close your eyes! You're asleep . . . sound asleep . . . you can still hear my voice, but you are asleep . . . sound, sound sleep . . . you are now in a deep, hypnotic sleep and will not awaken until I tell you to . . ."

The above is, of course, only a guide. It can be shortened or lengthened depending on the reaction of the subject. Watch his eyes. You will see them water and the eyelids will start to quiver when they are ready to close. Keep your voice soft and even. In effect you are singing a lullaby. Your words and syllables should have a regular monotony—a leisurely, monotonous, even rhythm.

Instead of having him gaze into your eyes you can hold some bright object for him to look at—a ring, a coin, a marble. I use one of the commercially-produced "Hypno-discs," which I find especially effective. You can even use your fingertip. Just hold your finger in front of, and slightly above, the subject and ask him to concentrate on the tip. Another method is to stand or sit facing the subject and to place your spread fingertips on each side of his .face, with your thumbs on his eyebrows against his nose. While giving the low, monotonous suggestions gently move your thumbs outwards from the nose, along the eyebrows, to the temples. Keep your fingers still at the sides of the subject's head and caress with your thumbs. The whole process should be extremely gentle.

If you find your first subject does not go to sleep, do

not worry about it. You may try quite a number before you get results.

However, should a subject suddenly open his eyes, grin, and say, "It didn't work!" you should still go through the waking up process. This is very simple. Before starting it remove any suggestions you may have made. If early in the session you told your subject that he could levitate, then do not forget to remove this suggestion before waking him, or he could step out of a fourth floor window later on!

Having removed your suggestions tell the subject that you are going to wake him. He is going to feel fine when he does wake; no headaches, no pains, no after-effects of any sort. He will feel completely refreshed and rested as though awakening from a full night's sleep. Tell him you will count to three and at "three" he will be wide awake. Start with, "One . . . starting to come out of it . . . feeling fine. Two . . . getting lighter and lighter . . . ready to wake. Three! Wide awake!" You can snap your fingers, clap your hands, or whatever, at "Three!" if you like.

I do not think it a good idea to bring the subject out of it too quickly, for instance by saying simply, "When I snap my fingers you will wake up!" This is too sudden and too much of a jolt to the nervous system. It is bad enough being rudely awakened in the morning by a strident alarm clock. You probably know how annoyed that can make you feel. To be suddenly snapped out of a hypnotic sleep feels much the same.

Should you plan on hypnotizing the same subject again at a future date then you can make things easier for yourself by giving a "password," or post-hypnotic suggestion. For instance, just before waking your subject you might say, "Next time I hypnotize you I will simply say the word 'galaxy' and you will immediately fall into a deep, hypnotic sleep. It will have no effect on you if someone other than me says the word; or if you hear my recorded voice, or my voice over the telephone, say the word. But if I am beside you in person, ready for a hypnotic session, I will only need to say that word 'galaxy' for you to fall into a deep, sound, hypnotic sleep."

Choose a word a little out of the ordinary for such a code word. It could be a little embarrassing if you had chosen a word like "martini" and then happened to be at a cocktail-party with your subject present. An unthinking remark on your part and at least one guest would appear to have had more than enough to drink!

Now that you can hypnotize, and "de-hypnotize," where does this generally accepted science fit into the occult; the supernatural? One place it fits is in mediumship. Hypnotism can help make a person a psychometrist, an astral traveler, a clairvoyant or, almost, what-you-will. Here is an experiment you can try. Hypnotize your subject. When he is in the somnambulistic stage tell him to go, in his astral body, out of the house, down the road and into the house of a friend—preferably someone you know but he does not. Tell him to describe his journey as he goes. He will start speaking and talk to you as though you and he were walking the route together. Your notes, or tape-recording, might go like this:

HYP.: "Where are you now?"
SUBJ.: "I am just going out of the front door . . . I am in the street."
HYP.: "Is it raining?"
SUBJ.: "No. It's quite dry."
HYP.: "Are there any cars parked outside?"
SUBJ.: "Yes. Two. A black Ford and a blue Chevy."
HYP.: "What are their license-plate numbers?"

And so on. Get a report on every part of the journey. When he reaches his destination ask him to describe it fully—the furniture, the wallpaper, the ornaments. Do not forget to bring him back to his body afterwards. When the session is over check the information obtained. It should all check out.

Have a séance. Start with a Ouija board or automatic writing. If you are getting good results ask the "spirit" if it will speak to you through a hypnotized person. The answer is invariably *Yes*. Hypnotize your subject. Then, when he is fully under, say: "I now want you to let someone else use your vocal chords. There is someone waiting there to talk to us and I want you to help him. It will only be for a limited time, and he will only use your voice. Now just relax, and let him try to speak. Relax . . . relax . . . Is there anybody there?"

If you cannot get the "spirit" to actually speak through your subject, and it is certainly not easy for all "spirits," (though many seem to have no problem at all) then let the subject act as a clairvoyant, or clairaudient, describing what he sees and relaying the messages. It will also be found that great ability in automatic writing is possible in a trance state; as in dowsing, scrying, and ESP.

A particularly interesting facet of hypnotism is age regression. This was especially brought to public notice in the Bridey Murphy case. Briefly, Morey Bernstein hypnotized a young housewife in Pueblo, Colorado, and took her back to re-live a previous life in Ireland. Subsequent to the appearance of his report on the experiment a Chicago newspaper published an "exposé," claiming everything described by the Irish Bridey Murphy had actually happened in this present life to the Pueblo housewife. Bernstein's later edition of his book amusingly exposes the "exposé" but, as is unfortunately so often the case, the exposé lives on in most people's minds. I would particularly recommend the New Edition of *The Search For Bridey Murphy*.

How can you experiment with age regression to investigate the possibilities of reincarnation? It must be done by going back in easy stages, step by step. Hypnotize your subject in your usual manner. Then go on: "I now want you to go back . . . go back in time to an earlier year . . . back, back . . . back to the time when you were ten years old. You are now ten years old . . . it is your tenth birthday . . . tell me about it. Describe your surroundings . . . where are you?"

After hearing about the subject's tenth birthday, take him back further. Ask him to describe when he was six. Then three. Then one.

Now for the big step: "You are now traveling further back in time . . . back to the time when you were six months old . . . but we are not stopping there. Back to your birth . . . and back even further . . . further and further back to a time long before your birth . . . back . . . back, to a previous life. You are in another time; another place . . . describe to me what you see . . ."

Do keep notes of all these experiments or, better still, tape-record them. I do not guarantee you will find another Bridey Murphy — though it is not impossible.

XIII

I CHING

The *I Ching,* or *Yi King,* is an ancient Chinese method of divination. Also known as the *Book of Changes,* it was in use two and a half millennium ago, and received high praise from no less a personage than Confucius himself. It is based on a "universal pattern of movement" which can be broken down into sixty-four separate and distinct stages. These in turn are each further broken down into six sub-stages.

Pronounced *Yee-Jing,* the Book does not purport to tell you what the future inevitably holds. Rather it suggests how to work to derive benefit from a possible situation, and how to avoid other impending situations and tragedies. The answers that it gives are very much to the point; not so dependent on interpretation as in so many other types of divination.

The correct, and traditional, method of divining is to use sticks, though coins can be used as I will show. The sticks, fifty in number, ideally should be yarrow stalks but in actual fact you can use wooden doweling. The length should be about eighteen inches and they should be stored in a lidded container. Before commencing it is advised that you place the Book on a cloth before you as you kneel facing North. The cloth, on which the Book rests, may in turn rest upon a table and should be in the center of the room. You should have incense at hand which you will light, after doing three ceremonial *kowtows* to start the ritual. Then take the sticks from their container and hold them in a bunch, horizontally, in your right hand. Rotating your hand clockwise, pass them through the smoke of the incense three times. As you do this concentrate hard on the question you are going to ask. Try not to ask any ambiguous question. Ask, rather, what will happen if . . . ? Why is such-and-such not happening? Should I do so-and-so? How should I do such-and-such? The sticks are now ready to operate. Answers to questions are given in what are called *hexagrams* and *moving lines*. Although seeming extremely complicated to start with, the whole rite can be quickly mastered.

Take any one of the sticks and put it back in the container. That one will not be used. The only reason for this is the very unsatisfactory word—tradition. You are left, then, with forty-nine sticks. These you bunch together and, still thinking hard on the question, slap your hand down on the table spilling the sticks and, with one finger, dividing them into two piles. This should be done in one quick movement so that you get two sets of sticks arbitrarily divided. Take one stick from the pile on your right and place it between the last two fingers of your left hand. Now, from the pile on your left, count off four sticks at a time until you are left with the remaining one, two, three, or full four. This remainder you place between the next two fingers of your left hand. Now do the same for the pile on your right, putting the remainder between the next two fingers. In your left hand you now have a total of five or nine sticks. Put them to one side.

Take up the remaining forty, or forty-four, sticks in your right hand, slamming them down again and dividing them as before. Again take one from the right-hand pile and put it between the last two fingers of your left hand. Again divide the left-hand pile in fours and take up the remainder; and divide the right-hand pile in fours and take up the remainder. This total will be either four sticks or eight. Put them to one side.

Go through the same procedure again with the remaining sticks, and again the resultant total in the left hand will be four or eight. These three totals indicate whether or not the bottom line of the answering hexagram will be "broken," and whether or not it is "moving." Possible combinations of numbers, and the types, are as follows:

COMBINATION	DESCRIPTION	LINE TYPE	RITUAL NUMBER
5 + 4 + 4	moving (Old Yang)	—0—	9
5 + 4 + 8	static (Young Yin)	— —	
5 + 8 + 4	static (Young Yin)	— —	8
5 + 8 + 8	static (Young Yang)	———	
9 + 4 + 4	static (Young Yin)	— —	
9 + 4 + 8	static (Young Yang)	———	
9 + 8 + 4	static (Young Yang)	———	7
9 + 8 + 8	moving (Old Yin)	—X—	6

When you have noted this number combination take all forty-nine of the sticks and do the three throwing-down-and-dividings again. You now have a second set of numbers; the line of the hexagram second from the bottom. Repeat the ritual until you have six sets of numbers; the complete hexagram. If there are any "moving" lines in the hexagram, according to the table, draw a second hexagram with these moving lines replaced by their opposites. In other words, an open moving line replaced by a closed line, and a closed moving line replaced by an open one. This might give you two hexagrams like this (fourth line, from the bottom upwards, "moving"):

	First Hexagram		Second Hexagram
9 + 4 + 8	———		———
9 + 4 + 4	— —		— —
9 + 8 + 8	— X —	changed to:	———
5 + 8 + 8	———		———
5 + 8 + 8	———		———
5 + 8 + 4	— —		— —

The text and Commentary of the Book will now give you the meaning of the First Hexagram, the moving line, and the Second, modified, Hexagram.

Using the sticks, in the manner described, can be slow and inconvenient, particularly if you have a "burning" question to ask. Instead of the sticks, then, it is possible to work out your hexagram using three coins. Shake the coins in your hands, as you would dice, and think of your question. Then throw them down on the ground or table. The coins should be of equal size and denomination and you interpret according to whether

they land showing "heads" or "tails." The Coin Table
is as follows:

COMBINATION	DESCRIPTION	LINE TYPE	RITUAL NUMBER
Tail + Tail + Tail	moving (Old Yin)	— X —	6
Tail + Tail + Head	static (Young Yin)	— —	7
Tail + Head + Head	static (Young Yang)	———	8
Head + Head + Head	moving (Old Yang)	—0—	9

Although so much quicker and more convenient, the
coin method is much frowned upon. It is felt, and I
agree whole-heartedly, that the ancient art of divination
is somewhat sacred and demands a certain respect and
ritual. It should be used only for questions of a serious
nature and consequently should be approached without
rushing and with due observance of the time-honored
rituals.

The various translations of the Yi Ching I give in the
Bibliography. I do particularly recommend the translation by Professor Richard Wilhelm and also John Blofeld's Introduction to his own translation.

MEDIUMS

A medium is a person through whom you may communicate with the spirits of the dead, either by making
use of the medium's own organism or by producing certain phenomena which, as yet, we are unable to explain (e.g. ectoplasm). These two types are known as
mental and *physical* mediums. Both types usually operate while in a trance state. The mental medium hears
or sees the spirits of the dead (clairaudience and clair-
voyance), and may also produce written messages
through automatic writing. The physical medium produces lights, materializations, knocks, levitation, etc.

Although the term *medium* dates from relatively re-
cent times we can find the origins of the profession in
the *sibyl* of ancient Greece, who served as intermediary
between the people and the priests on the one hand,
and the Gods themselves and the dead on the other.
The Bible's so-called "witch" of Endor (actually the
word *witch* does not appear in the text) was no more
than a medium, acting as a bridge between Saul and
Samuel.

In its modern sense *medium* infers a follower of the
spiritualist movement. Since the spiritualist's original
mediums, the Fox sisters in 1848, there have been but
a handful of outstanding mediums amongst a host of
frauds. It is unfortunate that it is so easy for an un-
scrupulous person to masquerade as a sensitive.

The Davenport brothers were two such imposters who
achieved great acclaim before their exposure. They
would sit inside a large cabinet and be bound to their
chairs by members of the audience. When the doors of

the cabinet were closed the audience would hear a great noise from inside; bells ringing, banjos strumming, tambourines rattling. On the doors being opened the instruments were found to be in their places on the floor and the two brothers still firmly tied to the chairs. It took two professional conjurers to expose the brothers for the tricksters that they were.

But honest, and extremely successful, mediums there have been. Perhaps the best known of these was Daniel Dunglas Home (1833–1886). Of the number of books and articles describing this man and his phenomena there is not a single word on any valid "exposure" of his methods. Never was he caught cheating at his séances. An almost equally important medium was Eusapia Palladino (1854– 1918), though a less spectacular personality than Home. Palladino was caught cheating on a few occasions but the vast majority of the time her investigators were so strict in their control that there was no possible chance of fraud.

Perhaps the most famous of Home's feats was his levitation, out of one window and in at another, seventy feet above the ground. It occurred at Ashley House, Victoria Street, London. Present were Lord Adare, the sporting young Irish peer, his cousin Captain Charles

Wynne, and the Honorable Master of Lindsay (later Earl of Crawford and Balcarres). Both Adare and Lindsay wrote separate accounts of what happened that evening. After a normal beginning to the séance—normal for Home's séances, that is—with telekinetic phenomena (the movement of objects without physical contact), and the appearance to Lindsay of an apparition, Home began to pace the floor. He was in a trance state, as he had been all evening. Home walked through to the next room and a window was heard to be raised. Lindsay states that he heard a voice whisper in his ear, telling him that Home would pass out of one window and in at another. The next moment they all saw Home floating in the air outside their window. There was no ledge of any sort between the two windows, which were nearly eight feet apart, and they were about seventy feet above the ground. Although there was no light in the room the moon provided sufficient illumination for all to distinguish each other and to see the furniture in the room quite clearly.

After remaining in position for a few seconds outside the window—with his feet about six inches above the window-sill—Home opened the window and "glided into the room feet foremost." Adare went to close the window in the other room and found that it had only been opened twelve to fifteen inches. Home was asked how he had managed to pass through so small a space, and replied by showing them. Adare describes it, ". . . he then went through the open space, head first, quite rapidly, his body being nearly horizontal and apparently rigid. He came in again, feet foremost; and we returned to the other room." Later, when Home came out of his trance, he was "much agitated; he said he felt as if he had gone through some fearful peril, and that he had a most horrible desire to throw himself out of the window."

Eusapia Palladino never managed any levitation as sensational as Home's, but levitation of objects she did do. One such occurred at a sitting with Camille Flammarion and Guillaume de Fontenay. Before the séance Flammarion made a detailed investigation of the room. He checked windows and doors, blinds, chairs, the sofa, everything. He looked for electric wires, batteries, any form of concealed mechanism, but found nothing. Before the séance Madame Zelma Blech, the hostess, stripped and searched the medium but found nothing suspicious. The sitting took place in full light and is comprehensively described by Flammarion in *Mysterious Psychic Forces* (London, 1907):

"The medium sits *before* the curtain, turning her back to it. A table is placed before her—a kitchen table, made of spruce, weighing about fifteen pounds. I examined this table and found nothing in it suspicious. It could be moved about in every direction.

"I sit at first on the left of Eusapia, then 'at her right side. I make sure as far as possible of her hands, and her feet, by personal control. Thus, for example, to begin with, in order to be sure that she should not lift the table either by her hands or her legs, or her feet, I take her left hand in my left hand, I place my right open hand upon her knees, and I place my right foot upon her left foot. Facing me, M. Guillaume de Fontenay, no more disposed than I to be duped, takes charge of her right hand and her right foot.

"There is full light. . . . At the end of three minutes the table begins to move, balancing itself, and rising sometimes to the right, sometimes to the left. A minute afterwards it is *lifted entirely from the floor*, to a height of about nine inches, and remains there two seconds.

"In a second trial, I take the two hands of Eusapia in mine. A notable levitation is produced, nearly under the same conditions. We repeat the same experiments thrice, in such a way that five levitations of the table take place in a quarter of an hour, and for several seconds the four feet are completely lifted from the floor, to the height of about nine inches. During one of the levitations the experimenters did not touch the table at all, but formed the chain above it and in the air; and Eusapia acted in the same way."

Levitation of a table was done at a number of séances through Eusapia Palladino. Many men of note, such as Professors Lombroso and Richet, attended such sittings, and at one de Fontenay succeeded in taking several photographs. These are quite remarkable, showing the very solid table in various stages of levitation. Thanks to the magnesium flash used for the pictures all details are to be seen, including the investigators' control of the medium.

Jack Webber, the Britisher mentioned in the chapter on Ectoplasm, is one of the few modern mediums capable of levitating objects. Although Webber works in darkness, infra-red photographs have shown a heavy table floating above ground lifted, apparently, by no more than a fine strand of ectoplasm coming from the medium.

Mental mediums are fairly plentiful; the most outstanding one of the present day being Arthur Ford. He it was who successfully broke the Houdini code—the cypher message left by Harry Houdini to his wife Beatrice when he died. It is not suggested that anyone try levitating out of a fourth floor window, in the manner of Home, nor even try levitating a table (though this may well be possible—see *Table Tipping*). But mental mediumship may well be within your reach, for everyone has "psychic power" to some degree. If you have success with tea-leaf reading, then you are displaying psychic power. If you operate a pendulum, you are using psychic power. As an automatic writer you are acting as a medium. Similarly as a crystal-gazer, or using a talking board, you are a medium—however slightly developed. How to go on to greater things? How to become another Arthur Ford? There are two possible systems of training open to you. The first especially involves lengthy training and dedication. Spasmodic effort is of no use.

To start with you need to be in good physical condition. You are trying to develop to the point where you can sit back and let the unconscious mind itself relax while another entity takes over. If your unconscious is forever worrying about putting on weight, smoking too much, drinking too much, headaches, pains, etc., then it is never going to be able to relax. Relaxation is the keyword in psychic development. Tension is anathema.

Hand in hand with relaxation goes breathing; correct breathing. The majority of people breathe shallowly, without ever really filling their lungs. Practice breathing deeply—not necessarily long breaths, but *deep* ones. Sit in a straight-backed, yet comfortable chair. Relax completely and breathe deeply and evenly. To anyone who has been hypnotized this may sound vaguely familiar. So it should, for relaxation and deep even breathing are a necessary prelude to hypnosis. In fact hypnosis is the second method of attaining mediumship, and is fully covered under its own heading.

When you have attained complete relaxation together with good breathing, then you may go on to concentration, the next step. True concentration is more difficult than you might think. I might give you an object, a woman's bracelet for example, and ask you to concentrate on it. After a few minutes I would take it back and ask you to describe it. I am sure the description you would give would be a good one, and reasonably accurate. But I wonder how many other bracelets it would fit? For in true concentration you are not just *looking* at the object, you are getting the *feel* of it. You almost reach the point—in fact many sensitives do reach the point—where you could describe who made the bracelet. You could describe exactly how it was made and give a complete physical description of the craftsman! This, in its extreme, is called *psychometry*.

How can you get close to this degree of concentration? Simply by practice. Sit down. Relax. Get into your rhythmic breathing. Then take some simple object, such as a plain gold ring, and study it. Look at it carefully, while continuing your deep breathing. (In fact your deep, rhythmic breathing should, by now, have become quite automatic—something you don't even have to think about.) First take in the overall shape of the ring; its basic design. Note its thickness, its weight. Is there any engraving on the ring? How deeply is it cut? Look at it from all angles. Note the smoothness of the metal; any scratches there might be. Is it highly polished or is it growing dull? Is it an old ring or a new one? How old, or how new? Feel it. Study it. Concentrate on it. Get to the point where you can close your eyes and still see it. Get to the point where you can put away the actual ring yet still study it in your mind's eye. See it in your mind and be able to turn it over and over; around and about. You may suddenly find that while examining the ring *in your mind* you notice some feature which had escaped your attention on the real ring. You will take the real ring to check—and find you are correct!

These steps should be taken slowly. They cannot be rushed. Just relaxing and breathing correctly may take several weeks. Practice of concentration may take several months. In fact there is no reason really why this should ever stop. Eventually, however, you will be at a stage where you can sit, perfectly relaxed, and let come into your mind whatever will, and be able to describe it exactly though never having seen it before. It may be an object or even a person. This is the time to start sitting with another person; up until now you have been working alone. Sit opposite a friend and ask him to just sit quietly, not thinking of anything in particular. You relax, as usual, and also try to think of nothing. You may, to start with, hold his hands in yours. As persons or objects come to your mind describe them, aloud. The sitter is to say nothing until the end of the experiment, for you want no unconscious guiding or prompting. It may well be, and frequently is, that by the time you reach this final stage you are slipping into a light trance as you relax. Indeed you may remember nothing of what you tell your sitter. This is as it should be, so do not get alarmed.

It is not within everyone to develop to the point of being an effective, and consistent, mental medium, but it is within a larger percentage than is generally supposed. If you feel drawn in this direction, do follow it up. And remember . . . relax!

XV

NUMEROLOGY

The basis of all numbers and calculations are the numbers 1 through 9. Pythagoras said, "The world is built upon the power of numbers." He it was who reduced the universal numerals to these nine primary ones. The method of reduction is simply to add. Any number, no matter how high, may thus be reduced. For example, the number 7,548,327 would be $7 + 5 + 4 + 8 + 3 + 2 + 7 = 36$, in turn further reduced to $3 + 6 = 9$. In this way all numbers can be reduced to a single one. The same holds true for letters and words; certain numerical values being given to the letters of the alphabet:

1	2	3	4	5	6	7	8	9
A	B	C	D	E	F	G	H	I
J	K	L	M	N	O	P	Q	R
S	T	U	V	W	X	Y	Z	

The numbers then have certain occult values attached to them, and are each associated with one of the nine planets. For example, 1—the letters A, J, and S—is associated with the Sun. It signifies leadership, creativity, positiveness. These values and associations will be dealt with fully below.

In Numerology dates and names are reduced to their primary numbers and then interpreted according to the values attributed to those numbers. In this way many things may be discovered. For instance, the type of job for which you are best suited; the geographical location likely to be the most harmonious for you; the marriage partner most suited to you. Your first job is to find your Birth Number and your Name Number.

BIRTH NUMBER

You were born on August 31st, 1942. To reduce this date to a single primary number you would write it 8.31.1942 and add: $8 + 3 + 1 + 1 + 9 + 4 + 2 = 28$; $2 + 8 = 10$; $1 + 0 = 1$. Your birth number is therefore 1. This represents the influences at the time of your birth. It is similar to, and should correspond in many ways, with your left hand (see chapter on *Palmistry*) and your Natal horoscope (see *Astrology*).

Your Birth Number is the one to consider when deciding upon dates for important events. In the above example, the signing of any contracts should be done on dates which also reduce to 1. Your planetary sign is the Sun, a *fire* sign. You would therefore be happiest married to someone whose sign is compatible, i.e. another fire sign, or an air sign: Sun, Jupiter, Mars, Uranus or Mercury—numbers 1, 3, 9, 4, 5.

The numbers, their planets and signs, are as follows:

Number	Planet	Sign
1	Sun	Fire
2	Moon	Water
3	Jupiter	Fire
4	Uranus	Air
5	Mercury	Air
6	Venus	Earth
7	Neptune	Water
8	Saturn	Earth
9	Mars	Fire

NAME NUMBER

The single primary number obtained from the numerical values of the letters of your name is the number which you will use most frequently. From the number/letter equivalency given above you can take a name, such as John F. Kennedy, and reduce it thus:

Name: JOHN F KENNEDY

Value: 1685   6   2555547   =   59   =   14   =   5

[Immediately you can see here the predominance of the number 5—in fact there are five of them—which is also the Name Number itself. Number 5 people make friends easily and get along well with persons of almost any other number. They are quick in thought and in decisions.]

The name you reduce in this way should be *the name most generally used*. For the late, famous, conjuror and escapologist Houdini, for example, you would use the one name HOUDINI rather than Harry, or Henry Houdini. HOUDINI gives the Name Number of 8—signifying "success." This Houdini certainly had, both materially and in his many attempts at doing the seemingly impossible.

An excellent example of marriage compatibility may be seen in the case of Napoleon and his empress Josephine:

NAPOLEON
51763565   = 38 = 11 = 2

JOSEPHINE
161578955   = 47 = 11 = 2

Both names reduce first to 11 and subsequently to 2. Josephine's beauty and grace of manner were certainly of great assistance to her husband in the establishment of his power. And while she shared his throne, from 1804 to 1809, their court was brilliant.

Let us look now at the value attached to the primary numbers.

1: SUN — Letters A, J, S.
Very much the driving life force. A leader. Ambitious. Tends to be impatient. The explorer. The extrovert. Automatically assumes command. Frequently a "big brother." Very strong feelings either for or against. Would not knowingly hurt anyone but might not realize his own strength. Can stand being praised and is entitled to it. Praise can spur him to greater things.

2: MOON — Letters B, K, T.
Sensitive, domestic. Tends to be emotional, and easily influenced to tears. Has a fertile imagination. Very fond of the home. Patriotic. Accepts changes in surroundings. Prefers to live near water. Often possesses musical talents and would make a very good medium.

3: JUPITER — Letters C, L, U.
The investigator; the scientist; the seeker. An interest in the material rather than the spiritual. Ideas on religion frequently change. Has a great sense of humor. Not greatly interested in money. Very trusting, yet likes to know the "why" and the "how."

4: URANUS — Letters D, M, V.
Inclined to appear strange and eccentric, because he is usually ahead of his time. Very interested in the occult; in psychic research. Inclined to anything out of the ordinary. Strong intuitive tendencies. Can be bitingly sarcastic if crossed. Believes in liberty and equality. Can usually pre-

dict the probable outcome of actions and businesses.

5: MERCURY — Letters E, N, W.
   Active, both physically and mentally. Inquiring, exploring. Fond of reading and researching. Good at languages. Would make a very good teacher, writer, secretary. Makes friends easily. Usually methodical and orderly; adept at simplifying systems.

6: VENUS — Letters F, O, X.
   Gentle and refined; pleasant and sociable. Usually good looking. Natural peacemaker; able to soothe ruffled feelings. Often experiences difficulty in financial fields. Excellent as a host or hostess. Friendly and agreeable.

7: NEPTUNE — Letters G, P, Y.
   Frequently possesses ESP; extremely "psychic." Introvert. Although he does not say much he usually knows a great deal. Mysterious. Often interested in psychology, psychiatry, chemistry and botany. Knowledgable in astrology and all fields of the occult. Fond of fishing. Inclined to take from the "Haves" and give to the "Have-nots."

8: SATURN — Letters H, Q, Z.
   Inclined to be cold and pessimistic. Not much sense of humor. Often slow getting off the mark but usually ends up ahead of the game. Successful especially where money is concerned. Frequently connected with mining, real estate and the law. Also with cemeteries and pawn-shops. Believes that hard work never killed anyone. Often prepossessed with thoughts of the past.

9: MARS — Letters I, R.
   Very emotional. Can be extremely jealous. Active,

though ruled by emotions. Tied very much to family background. Loyal. Apt to be suspicious of strangers. Impulsive. Tends to be afraid of the unknown. Often associated with surgery; physical and mental illnesses.

You are all set, then, to study a friend from the numerological point of view. Suppose your friend is named Jane Doe. She was born on June 23rd 1947. She is planning on moving into a new apartment in Trenton, New Jersey, sometime in November 1968. What can you tell her and advise her? Take it step by step. .

First of all work out her Birth Number:
  June 23rd, 1947 = 6.23.1947 = 32 = 5

Then her Name Number:
  JANE   DOE
  1155   465 = 27 = 9

Armed with these two important numbers what can you say? First of all look at the girl herself—number 9. She can be very emotional, and very jealous. She tends to be impulsive; is tied very much to her family background; is suspicious of strangers and afraid of the unknown. From these last two facts you know that it has taken her quite a little soul-searching to reach the decision to move into a new apartment. At the same time, being impulsive she feels that having made the decision the sooner she makes the move the better. Her new apartment will in some way reflect her family background. Perhaps in the way it is decorated, perhaps in the type of building it is in. Should she decide to have a room-mate you should suggest someone whose Name Number is compatible with her *fire* sign, i.e. someone with the Name Number 1, 3, 4, 5, or 9.

111

Now to look at where she is moving and when.

TRENTON NEW JERSEY
2955265   555   159157 = 77 = 14 = 5.

The number of the geographical location is the same as her Birth Number. This should be an ideal place for her. One which will truly give the feeling of "home."

She plans to move sometime in November, 1968. November is the eleventh month, $11.1968 = 26 = 8$

You need, then, to add a day which will bring the total to 5, to agree with her Birth Number. November 6th, 15th, or 24th are, then, the most propitious days:

$$11.6.1968 = 32 = 5$$
$$11.15.1968 = 32 = 5$$
$$11.24.1968 = 32 = 5$$

You could even go on to suggest how she should decorate the apartment so far as colors are concerned, for there is an affinity of colors and numbers:

1 — brown, yellow, gold.
2 — green, cream, white.
3 — mauve, violet, lilac.
4 — blue, gray.
5 — *light* shades of any color.
6 — all shades of blue.
7 — *light* shades of green and yellow.
8 — dark gray, blue, purple, and black.
9 — red, crimson, pink.

You would like to give her a record as a house-warming gift? Her taste in music can be taken from Numerology. According to Cheiro, probably the greatest numerologist of them all, number 1 people like inspiring, martial music, as do number 3 and number 9. Number

112

2 and number 7 people prefer wind and string instruments. The violin, the 'cello, the harp, the clarinet and flute. Number 4 people, together with 8, enthuse over choral arrangements, organs and religious music generally. Number 5 people are far from "square." They like something a little different; be it psychedelic; *musique concrete;* or dixieland-cum-rock-and-roll. Number 6 people are the romantics, preferring sweet music with lilt and rhythm.

It is possible to go on and on. You can check your health through Numerology. You can find the most effective herbal cures. You can pick the potential winner of a horse race, a football or a baseball game. You can probably work out the license plate numbers of cars most likely to run you down! Numerology is a fascinating science; and one which can give you endless entertainment, whether you believe in it or not.

XVI

PALMISTRY

Palmistry, or Cheiromancy (after Cheiro, the great palmist), is a means of divination whose origin is lost in history. It was common during Medieval times and is known to have existed when Greece and Rome were at their height. From the scattered information we have of Celtic Europe there is some reason to believe that there too the hand was considered to reflect its owner. As with other types of divination there is a fixed set of meanings to learn—in this case the map of the hand and the meanings of the lines. There is also the need for some carefully applied intuition.

The hand changes throughout your life. The lines you see in your palm now are not quite the same as were there a year ago, and probably very different from five years ago. Although your hand gives an outline of ·your life it is only a *tentative* outline. You yourself will have the final decision on the course your life will take. Whether you want the position or not, you are the captain of your soul.

Palmistry, like any other kind of divination or like even a doctor's examination, is strictly a *diagnostic* reading. It can point out the forces that operate within yourself or within another, and it can point out the logical results of these forces. You as a person can accept them as they are or begin to change them. Your own hand, by the way, can serve as a handy "reference book" for reading the palms of others, but you will not gain much from trying to read your own palm. This should be left to another—perhaps a friend who is familiar with the art and who can be trusted to be honest with you. You are far too close to yourself to really have an objective view of your own personality.

When you read the palms of others always consider the meanings of the lines you see before you speak. Some lines may show a particular area in which your subject has very serious problems: this should be presented to him as "an area of possible weakness and something for which you should be particularly watchful." On a few occasions you may encounter that peculiar combination of lines which indicates a premature death. If this is the case by no means come out bluntly with what you see. Rather, emphasize the need for great care in the future to avoid illness, accidents, violence, or whatever the rest of the hand may seem to imply as possible causes. Do remember: palmistry is only diagnostic. It is never a final pronouncement.

If you take up palmistry, even as an amusement, remember that you also take up a responsibility. For a few minutes you will be an "authority figure." Whether or not it is apparent at the time, your words will have far greater power than before. Others will listen to what you say and will, within themselves, consider your words very carefully. As a palmist your attitude is of great importance. Never try to "second guess" your subject by adding on-the-spot observations and facts you may know beforehand but which are not shown in the palm. Ideally you should know nothing whatsoever of the person you are working with. The hands and your (the palmist's) intuition should be enough. If you take up palmistry you will find that a comparison of the person with the palm will be very interesting indeed. Perhaps at times your reading of someone's palm may not seem entirely correct. This is nothing to worry about. Occasionally you will miss—but more often the match will be amazingly close and detailed.

Any time you're meeting someone for the first time you can pick up a tentative (and often useful) first impression of his personality by unobtrusively glancing at the lines of his hand. One who often reads the palms of others soon notes the interesting fact that, while few will profess to specifically believe in the art, everyone is interested and more than willing to hear what the palmist has to say.

FIRST OBSERVATION

Different palmists have different ways of working, for this is a very individual sort of art. Some will explain each step to the subject, discussing the reason for every observation. Others will merely report what they see. The following is based on the former method of operation, although any way of reading the palm is likely to follow a similar pattern.

The shape of the hands is useful to note at first, although you should mention it last and in the context of your other observations. Generally a person with long, articulate hands and fingers will tend toward the contemplative and the artistic, while one with short, broad fingers and hands will tend to enjoy doing things and enjoying life without particular concern for deeper meanings.

For a right-handed person, the left hand shows what he was born with—the traits and habits, as well as the course his life would have taken had things gone as they were when he was born.

This individual's right hand shows what he has *done* with his life so far. Someone who has constantly tried to improve his lot and avoided leaning on others is likely to have quite a difference between his two palms. For a subject who is left-handed the roles of left and right, or unconscious and conscious respectively, will be reversed. It is best to begin first with the hand that shows what one was born with, and what still is in the unconscious.

If the lines of the hand are deep and clear they indicate a person who experiences and understands much of the pain and the joy his life will encounter. If, however, the lines of the palm are faint and very light, their owner will tend to be rather superficial and color-

116

less. He would gain much by getting out and enjoying life.

A line which is in the form of a "chain" indicates a weakness in that which the line symbolizes. More attention will be needed.

Many lines can indicate a very complex person. Indeed, the more experienced you become the more frustrated you may become! For you will soon realize how much you do not know. A subject with a detailed and intricate story in his palms always proves to be a tantalizing study and there always seems to be just a little bit more, hidden in obscure lines, which is just beyond your ken.

You will occasionally encounter the rare case where one of the lines branches or seems to have a parallel to itself. Often a closer look will show the parallel or branch to merely be part of another major line. If it is not, however, you will have the rare condition in which your subject has alternate courses open to him in his life. In such a case you should pick out that which seems better and encourage him to follow it.

The Line of Life (see figure 5)

The Life line is the major line on the hand; it indicates in general terms something of the course your life will take. As the illustration shows, the Life line curves about the thumb. At the very beginning it usually is joined with the line of the head, and the point at which the life and head lines separate indicates the relative time at which you became emotionally independent of your parents. If the two lines are never in contact at the beginning a very independent sort of person is indicated.

The life line is the only one on the hand which can be divided into an approximate scale of years, and as such it can be used to foretell major events to within a year or two of their happening. Taking a very soft

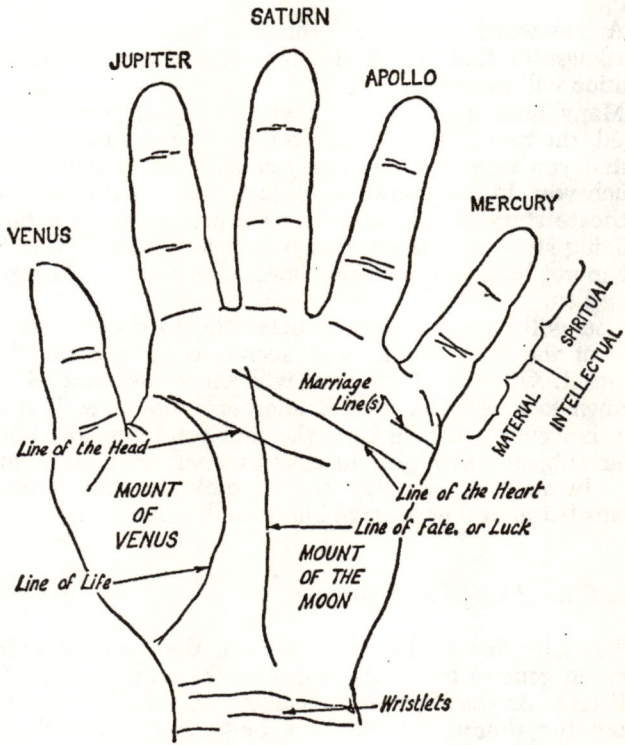

SATURN
JUPITER
APOLLO
MERCURY
VENUS

SPIRITUAL
INTELLECTUAL
MATERIAL

Marriage Line(s)

Line of the Head

MOUNT
OF
VENUS

Line of the Heart

Line of Fate, or Luck

MOUNT
OF THE
MOON

Line of Life

Wristlets

Fig. 5

pencil, divide your life line into three equal sectors. The first sector (including that portion which is merged with the head line) will count for twenty-five years and can be subdivided accordingly as you read a palm. The same will apply for the second and third sectors, though the third should be a little condensed.

A deep, clear, life line running smoothly around its

118

full length betokens a rich, full life with good health throughout. A line which is in the form of a chain shows probable poor health. If the line is chained in its latter portions the subject should beware of bad health in his later years.

A parallel to the life line on the side of the Mount of Venus shows useful luck and natural vitality working for the subject. This is always a good sign.

On most palms you will note that there are a number of tiny lines which run from the line of the head to the life line. Each of these indicates a goal of some kind which will be attained. If you work out the above time scale carefully you should be able to tell within two years when a major event will happen. What will they be? That, unfortunately, is beyond palmistry.

About two-thirds of the way down the life line will, at times, be a triangle formed by two short, minor, lines and a part of the life line itself. If this triangle (which can be of varying size) is present then a talent of some sort is possessed—some kind of art from which the subject can gain considerable personal satisfaction. If the talent is not immediately apparent to him, let him search around a little and examine his interests. It will be there.

An angle or sudden change of direction in the life line shows that there will be a change of course in the life. Calculate and note the approximate date. Care should be taken at this time in life, for the manner of living will change radically!

Similarly, a branch in the line of life indicates that, at the point in time where the branch occurs, the subject's life can take either of two courses. It is a matter for consideration and careful planning, for ultimately only he can determine and control the course his life will take.

A break in the life line will mean trouble, and if the break occurs in both hands it can be fatal unless great care is taken. If, however, a new line begains outside the break, or is a parallel to the life line and continues

119

unbroken along the Mount of Venus, the trouble will not be too drastic.

THE HEAD AND THE HEART

Note the relative lengths of the heart and head lines, for this will tell whether the subject tends towards things intellectual or whether he leans on the emotions and their very useful adjunct, intuition. For many people these lines are nearly equal in length; for others there will be more or less difference. Here the palmist should use his judgment as to just how important this difference will be.

The Line of the Head

The line of the head shows, by its length and depth, the intellectual capability of the subject. As mentioned above, the lines of head and heart should always be considered together, for the two can give insight into the very important relationship between the mind and the emotions.

A long, deep, and clear head line shows a clear, strong intellect that can be of great value to the person possessing it. If the head line is very long but slants downwards rather than across you will have the case of someone who has quite a high intelligence but tends to use it for the wrong goals—he may be along the "left-hand path." Such a person can be quite powerful. Guide him to better things if you can; but don't cross him!

On rare occasions you will meet someone whose heart and head lines join to form a single deep line which cuts directly across the palm. Such a person is always an interesting study, for here the head and heart are united and few barriers can stand before one whose intellect and intuition are so in line. Such an individual will probably be a genius, whether or not he knows it. (He usually does!) However, he should always keep tight control and close discipline on his mind, for here there is but a slight barrier between the strong, controlled mind and the uncontrolled chaos of mental unbalance. He is like a boat with a very powerful engine: magnificent performance is possible, but great care must be taken.

The Line of the Heart

The line of the heart shows, by its length and depth, the strength of your emotional and intuitive capabilities. As mentioned before, it should always be considered along with the head line as the relation between these two is an important one.

Someone who has a deep and long heart line is likely to feel deeply both the good and the bad, the joy and the sorrow, of his or her life. The emotions will be important to such a person, and judgment and hunches are likely to give valuable results.

It is interesting to note that nowadays many will have a stronger heart line on the left (or unconscious) hand than on the right (or conscious). In such a case the head line will be better developed in the right hand. The reason is simple—modern civilization, for better or for worse, emphasizes the intellect over the heart.

The Line of Fate

The line of fate (some prefer to call it the line of luck) does not occur in every hand. Its length and depth will show just how much good fortune you may have. For some this line will run strong and deep from the wrist to the middle finger. For such a person luck will come readily and freely, and he will do well without much effort. For the great majority, however, the luck line will be weak or nonexistent . . . any "luck" will only come through hard work!

The line of luck can give you some very valuable insights into personality flaws which are not usually apparent on the surface. For example, the line may be deep and unbroken up to the line of the heart, then break or disappear entirely at this point. A person with such lines would let emotions obstruct much of the good fortune that would normally come his way. Whether or not he realized it, worrying, fear, temper, and the like, would be limiting him. A little advice on this point can be very valuable indeed.

Similarly, a fate line breaking or terminating at the line of the head indicates an individual who "gets in his own way" by being over-cautious and thinking things over too much. When he has finally made up his mind the opportunity is past and nothing is gained. Each of these problems can be overcome by watching for them and correcting them before they do harm.

Someone whose line of luck starts over on the Mount of the Moon will probably have a peaceful and pleasing life. The old tradition is that he or she will be "happy without trying." If the line starts at the wristlets wealth will be inherited, or a rewarding career gained.

If the line of fortune branches near the bottom with one branch running over into the Mount of the Moon, good fortune will come in the form of a marriage or other attachment.

The Marriage Line

Feminine friends of the palmist are apt to be most interested in the marriage lines, which occur (appropriately enough) above the beginning of the heart line. The subject will probably have more than one such line. Possibly as many as four or five. It should be mentioned that the so-called marriage lines do not necessarily indicate so many marriages *per se*. They are rather the markers of loves, past and future, that stir the heart deeply. They will be sweet or bittersweet episodes she will remember throughout her life.

Each individual line will show by its depth and length

122

just how deeply someone quite special has left a mark. A very approximate time scale can be derived by noting whether the marriage line in question is near the heart line (early in life) or near the joint of the finger (later in life).

The Wristlets

The wristlets at the base of the hand can be a very general indication of how long the life will probably last. Each complete, well-formed, wristlet shows a complete and full twenty years. But the wristlets will change considerably throughout life, and choices and way of living will be the final factor in determining just how long this life will be.

The Mount of Venus

The thumb and its base are under the influence of Venus. The base, or Mount of Venus, can give an interesting picture of the warmth, kindness, and affection which are in the subject.

If the mount is warm, rounded, full, and firm he is under Venus' best influences: pleasing as a friend, delightful in love, and a person whose kindness to others always brings a warm response.

If, on the other hand, the Mount of Venus is thin, dry, and leathery he is a person who is cold and thin-lipped, tolerating little warmth toward others and receiving little or nothing in return . . . but don't tell him this! Say, instead, that he should loosen up, and learn to like others!

Often you will note that Venus' mount is crossed with many vertical and horizontal lines. Here will be a person who, for all else that his palm says, is not as serene as he appears on the surface. Underneath there are cross-currents of emotion which he feels deeply, but which he keeps hidden.

The Mount of the Moon

From most ancient times the moon has been linked with the psychic, and thus it is in palmistry. A triangle on this mount will indicate some natural talent in occultism. Any lines which arise here will have in them a hint of unconscious magic and of its close relation, love between man and woman.

Lines reaching towards the Mount of the Moon from around the edge of the hand will be a prediction of journeys by sea or air.

Finally, the firmness and fullness of this mount indicates generally just how well the subject can combine practicality with imagination.

THE FINGERS

As shown in the diagram each finger is associated with an astrological sign and is an indicator of the good, and bad, aspects of that sign. At the base of the finger is the "mount" associated with the sign of the finger. The fullness or thinness of the mount shows how strongly that particular sign affects the individual.

As the diagram shows, each finger is in turn divided into *three sections* to show the relative spiritual, intellectual, and material development under each of the astrological signs: Jupiter, Saturn, Apollo, and Mercury. If, for example, the lowest digit of the small finger (Mercury) is notably larger and more developed than the finger's other two digits, then there would be strength especially in management and salesmanship. Similar traits can be derived, using judgment and intuition with the astrological characteristics below, for each of the other signs.

Jupiter—Index Finger

The "father image," the boss, the commander, the leader, the executive.

Principle traits of this sign are pride, ambition and confidence.

124

Saturn—The Middle Finger

The wise old man, often a personification of old age and the very end of life.
Principle traits of this sign are wisdom, solitude, shyness, melanchology, and solitary bleakness.

Apollo—The Third Finger

The sun, all things bright and good, the arts, medicine. The principle trait of this sign is love of beauty.

Mercury—The Small Finger

Sharpness and quickness of mind, cleverness, shrewdness.
Principle traits of this sign are buoyance, friendliness, skill in management and commerce.

Study your own hands and see if you can form some tentative conclusions. Remember that every sign will have its good traits and its bad ones. Spend some time reading about the above signs in a book on Astrology. But above all read the palms of others, using knowledge backed by intuition, for this is the very best way to learn.

The art of reading the palm, then, is an ancient means of divination that has never grown old. Its accuracy, and accounts of previous readings by the palmist, are fresh items for conversation at any time. Even in our modern technological civilization someone who can read palms invariably finds himself at the center of any gathering. Skepticism will be put aside for a while and your words judged and considered. And even if you yourself are a skeptic under your façade of the occasion, still you will find moments of wonderment at some heretofore unknown fact you discover, or at some estimate of character which you suddenly find is in fact the truth.

XVII

PLANCHETTE

The planchette was invented in France. Basically it is a small platform mounted on casters so that it is free to move in any direction. Its shape is really immaterial, though when used on a talking board it may have a point to it which will indicate the particular letter of the message being received. In the commercially produced Ouija Board the planchette has a small, round, window of clear plastic holding what looks remarkably like a carpet tack as pointer. The window is supposed to show the letter indicated when it stops above it. In addition to this window this particular planchette is pointed at one end. As I mention in the chapter on Talking Boards, this can cause some slight confusion when the window indicates one letter on the lower of the two lines, and the pointer indicates another on the upper line. The three feet are felt-covered, to allow easy gliding on the smooth-surfaced board.

A planchette used for automatic writing, or drawing, usually has the ball-bearing type casters; two in number. In place of the third is the point of a pencil or ball-point pen, protruding through the platform. A planchette for use either with one of the commercially produced talking boards or with the layout suggested in the Talking Board chapter (in lieu of the upturned wine glass) can be easily constructed. Plywood, balsa wood, fiberboard, plexiglass; practically any material can be used for the platform. There is a school of thought that says the planchette must be of wood, but this is a fallacy. For the regular, pointing-type planchette a triangular shape is perhaps best, and easiest to construct. It should be an equilateral triangle with sides of approximately six inches. For the feet, use the self-sticking felt pads available at any dime store or hardware store.

For the automatic-writing planchette again you can use any material. Here, though, I would recommend wood simply because it will be easier to fix the feet and drill the hole for the pencil. Shape again can be triangular; you might make it slightly larger, say with eight inch sides. If you prefer it circular, then about eight inches in diameter. The two feet should be of the small, ball-bearing casters, securely fastened to the platform. At the apex of the triangle drill a hole that will make a tight fit for a pencil. Personally I prefer to use a ball-point pen, since it does not have to be removed for periodic re-sharpening. But this is up to you.

Decoration is a personal choice. The wood can be given a coat of clear varnish, or stained. I have seen home-made planchettes with mystic symbols carefully painted on them (it doesn't make them work any better!). I have seen them "antiqued;" I have seen them just plain wood. I have seen one—used by a witch acquaintance—in scarlet plexiglass, with a gold-leafed broomstick emblazoned on it! Here is one place where you can really let your imagination run wild. The first time you use your home-made planchette, why not ask the "spirit" what it thinks of it?

XVIII

PSYCHOMETRY

Many people are capable of doing psychometry—even though they do not know what the word means! It is the art of delineating the character, surroundings and influences of an article, or even a person. I say the "art" rather than the "gift" because, as you will see, it is something which you can learn to do. You can learn to pick up an object, such as a ring or a bracelet, and describe not only who owns it but who made it; in what surroundings it was made; in what surroundings it is usually kept, and many other things about it.

Impressions received may vary in intensity, dependant on the acuteness of the atmosphere which has affected the object. For example, my wife once received a letter from a young girl, to whom she had sent some small gift. It was a straightforward "thank you" letter. I did not know the girl, or any of the circumstances surrounding her. Taking the letter and concentrating on it I received a clairvoyant picture of a girl about nine years old. She was blonde, with her hair down to her shoulders, and with bangs. She was standing in a garden and seemed to me to be wearing long, white socks. My wife had never met the girl but spoke with a friend who knew the girl's family well. The girl was actually ten years old. She was indeed fair-haired, wearing it shoulder length and with bangs. She loved the small garden behind her house and spent much of her time there. What I had taken to be long, white socks were actually bandages. It seems she had been badly burned on the legs a short time before writing the letter. This, incidentally, was my very first try at psychometry.

Another example is of a psychometrist who was, as a test, handed a sealed package. After a moment he said that he felt he was in a very small room and that he could not see out of the windows. The package, he said, contained a green book which explained this room. He added that he felt extremely worried. The package actually contained the log-book of a small boat that used to travel between England and Ireland. The book had green covers and its last entry was written by the Captain as he strained to see through a thick fog that enveloped the boat and the small, enclosed bridge where he stood. Needless to say the Captain was quite worried, situated as he was in the busy shipping lane.

The steps, in learning to psychometrise, are easy ones requiring only practice, with patience. Take eight or ten samples of different substances: cloth of various types, leather, fur, wood, metal, stone, etc. Sit quietly and, taking one object at a time in your hands, concentrate on it. Feel its texture. Think of its origins. Try to picture the tree from which the wood came; the animal from which the fur came; and so on. Some people find they get their best results holding the object in one hand, some in the other. Some people prefer to hold the object to their forehead. Experiment. See which is best for you. Work at the objects regularly, spending as long as you feel comfortable on each object, but always going right through the complete set. It may be that you will get very definite impressions right away. But if you do not, continue as follows.

After a few weeks of the initial exercise place the objects each in an envelope. Have all the envelopes the same so that, outwardly, there is no way of telling one from another. Number them. Go through the concentration again regularly, this time trying to pick up a clue regarding the contents of the envelope. You may guess the object itself or you may get an impression of its origins—the sort of thing on which you were concentrating before. Write down your impressions of the contents in a notebook, against the numbers on the envelopes. After a few days, or weeks—depending on how often you practice—you may show a score something like the table on page 130.

ACTUAL CONTENT	ENVELOPE NUMBER	GUESSES						
		1	2	3	4	5	6	7
COTTON	A	silk	cotton	silk	wool	cotton	cotton	cotton
SILK	B	cotton	silk	velvet	silk	silk	cotton	silk
VELVET	C	wool	feather	bamboo	velvet	wool	velvet	oak
SNAKESKIN	D	ivory	feather	snakeskin	oak	feather	snakeskin	feather
SEASHELL	E	oak	ivory	shell	ivory	shell	shell	ivory
WOOL	F	shell	oak	velvet	wool	wool	iron	wool
IVORY	G	feather	shell	ivory	ivory	ivory	shell	shell
CLAY	H	iron	iron	clay	velvet	feather	clay	clay
IRON	I	velvet	snakeskin	ivory	iron	silk	bamboo	iron
BAMBOO	J	oak	velvet	bamboo	oak	bamboo	oak	oak
OAK	K	oak	wool	oak	oak	oak	bamboo	bamboo
FEATHER	L	clay	wool	cotton	velvet	snakeskin	feather	feather

You can see that there is a certain pattern emerging. By the (in this example) seventh try you can get fifty per cent correct. Others are very close. For instance, the two words, Oak and Bamboo, are frequently confused; as are Snakeskin and Feather.

Keep on with these sealed envelopes. Then introduce others. When you feel you are keeping a good, consistent score try your hand at other unsealed objects. A friend's ring, for instance. A letter, a photograph, a watch. As you hold the objects start by thinking of them in themselves. Then ask yourself, who has handled them most? Where did they come from? When were they made? Practice all the time. Such an item as a coin has usually passed through too many different hands to have gathered any positive *aura*. Concentrate more on objects of an individual nature. Whenever possible check on the results you achieve and keep a written record of them. In this way you can watch your progress.

The above exercises can be done quite well in a group. You can even arrange two teams and see which is the more accurate. Other exercises and tests will suggest themselves. Keep trying. Do not be discouraged . . . and keep those notes.

XIX

RADIESTHESIA

Basically Radiesthesia is the science of the pendulum. Its history can be traced back over 5,000 years, to the ancient races of the Orient. The pendulum really came to the fore, however, in the late Middle Ages, and again in the twentieth century. It is often used today in diagnosing disease in man, animals and plants, and in prospecting and various fields of research.

Virtually anyone can use a pendulum. In the Middle Ages a key on the end of a chain, or a ring on a silken thread, were popular. The ring is still much used today though commercially produced pendulums of wood, plastic and brass are generally available. You can make a very good one by using a fishing-weight or a plumb-bob.

To use a pendulum hold the thread, or chain, between the thumb and forefinger of your right hand (left hand if left-handed). On the table in front of you place a piece of paper, about three inches square, with a cross marked on it. One line of the cross should be marked YES and the other NO:

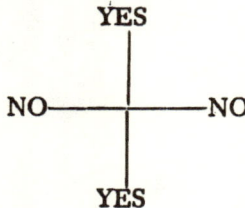

```
              YES
               |
               |
NO ————————————+———————————— NO
               |
               |
              YES
```

Rest your elbow on the table and allow sufficient thread for the pendulum weight to hang one to two inches above the surface of the paper. The weight should be directly over the center of the cross. Do not grip the thread too tightly. Hold your arm and hand perfectly still, so that the pendulum will not swing.

Now ask the pendulum a question. One which can be answered YES or NO. *Do not try to make the pendulum swing.* Yet although you try to hold your hand still, it will swing along one of the lines on the paper, thus giving an answer to your question. You do not need to ask the question aloud; you can just think it. Should the pendulum swing around in a circle, rather than indicating a definite YES or NO, then either your question was ambiguous and needs rephrasing, or else the answer cannot be given for some reason. Although you do not consciously make the pendulum swing it is obviously the muscles in your hand, or fingers, that cause it, acting unconsciously. What directs it—gives the particular answer? As with the talking board, automatic writing, etc., we do not know. Your guess is as good as mine.

As with the talking board a list of questions can be written out beforehand. If there is a group of you then take turns to be the Operator. It is possible to receive messages, again as with the talking board. Instead of the YES/NO piece of paper use a piece with the letters of the alphabet written out in the form of a half-circle. Due to the restricted swing of the pendulum the radius of the half-circle will have to be small. Consequently the letters will also have to be small. The messages will be spelled out by the pendulum swinging over the let-ters to indicate them.

A variation—a sort of pendulum version of table-tipping—is to have a water glass standing upright on the table and suspend the pendulum so that its weight hangs just inside it. In answer to questions the pendulum will swing until its weight strikes the side of the glass. One "chink" for YES; two for NO. One for A, two for B, three for C, etc.

The pendulum can be used for divining, or dowsing,

much as the forked hazel twig is. A hollow pendulum is used here, so that the *witness*—the sample of what is being sought—can be placed inside. If you are looking for gold, a piece of gold is put inside the pendulum; if water, the pendulum is filled with water, and so on. Having indicated the site of the material sought, the depth at which it will be found is indicated in any one of a number of ways. You can ask the depth—counting off and seeing it swing, or spin, when you reach the correct number. You can hold it over a piece of paper giving different depths and it will indicate the correct one. Or you can use the water glass method, the weight tapping the side of the glass the number of times that the material is feet deep.

One of the joys of the pendulum is that it is not necessary to leave the comfort of your own home in order to dowse for water, to follow a trail, to find a lost or stolen article, or even to diagnose someone else's illness. The idea behind this is that the pendulum indicates on a small scale what is happening at a' distance. For any of these things it is as well to use a pendulum with a definite point to it—rather than a ball type, or a ring. Sit at a table with a map before you, of the place to be dowsed. The larger the scale the better. Then, move the pendulum slowly across the map, in the same pattern you would follow if you were walking it on the spot. When you "reach" the site of the material the pendulum will indicate it by swinging rapidly in a circle, or by spinning around. Again you can go on to find the depth of the material below the surface. Mark the spot indicated on the map, and there you are!

A similar procedure is followed when looking for lost, or stolen, property. If you know roughly where it was lost then draw a sketch map of the area, the house, or the room. Again move the pendulum systematically about, while concentrating your thoughts on the missing object. Again you will get the rotating indication of where the object is.

To follow a trail, move your pendulum slowly along the roads as shown on the map. At each crossroads the pendulum will indicate which is the right one to take. In this manner, on a map, you can easily trace a route from A to B simply by concentrating on your destination, even if you have never been to B before.

The science of diagnosis by radiesthesia I will not deal with fully here. Basically it involves holding the pendulum over a smear of blood, belonging to an ailing person, and indicating a list of possible ailments. Violent reaction from the pendulum indicates the correct diagnosis. You then pass on to a list of the likely cures and again the correct one is indicated. The accuracy of this mode of diagnosis and cure is, in many places, open to some question.

XX

SCRYING

Crystal gazing, mirror gazing, water gazing, ink gazing—all these come under the general heading of *scrying*. Basically it is no more than a form of self-hypnosis. The most popular method is with a crystal ball: a sphere of genuine crystal about three or four inches in diameter, which should be free of any imperfections. A perfect crystal of this type is generally extremely expensive and so a sphere of glass is often substituted.

Recently balls of "Optical Acrylic Plexiglass" have appeared on the market. These are very good if they are carefully looked after, but they scratch very easily indeed.

The Abbot Trithemius, a mystic of the Middle Ages, gave explicit directions for scrying with a crystal: "Procure of a lapidary good, clear, pellucid crystal, of the size of a small orange, that is about one inch and a half in diameter; let it be globular or round each way alike; then, when you have got this crystal fair and clear, without any clouds or specks, get a small plate of pure gold to encompass the crystal round one half; let this be fitted on an ivory or ebony pedestal. Let there be engraved a circle round the crystal." He then gave certain astrological directions in connection with the art, such as the most propitious time and place for the practice, according to the positions in the heavens of the various planets.

One of the most famous of seers was Dr. John Dee, an English mathematician, alchemist, and astrologer. He was born in 1527 and died in 1608. In his earlier life he successfully devoted his time to mathematical and astronomical studies. However in the reign of Mary he was imprisoned on suspicion of practicing the "black art." Later, in the reign of Elizabeth I, he regained favor and worked for the Queen at a fixed salary. In the late sixteenth century he visited various foreign countries with his assistant Kelly. He was especially skilled in scrying and used either a small, perfect, crystal or natural black volcanic glass known as obsidian. This mirror, or *speculum*, is preserved in the British Museum. Other magicians, of the Ceremonial type, gave their instructions; usually involving the enclosure of the lower half of the crystal in gold, suitably inscribed with numerous magical symbols.

It was said that the operator should fast and pray for the few days immediately preceding the inspection of the crystal. He should make frequent ablutions and subject himself to strict religious discipline. During the invocation the operator was to face the East and summon, from the crystal, the spirit he desired to speak with. All this was to be done in such a Magic Circle as described in the article on Ceremonial Magic.

All these elaborate preparations and rituals are actually quite unnecessary. To successfully scry it is important to have the right attitude of mind, to be in the right mood, yes. But the elaborate rituals of the Ceremonialists are not called for. First of all choose a room where you will not be disturbed. Late evening is the best time. You should have absolute silence—no sound of traffic, radios, television, etc. Burn a little incense. It will help set the mood and will also aid concentration. Sit, comfortably, in a straight-backed chair with the crystal on a table before you. The crystal should lie on a large piece of black velvet, so that when you look at it there is nothing else within range which is likely to distract you. If you wish, instead of having the crystal on the table you can hold it, on its velvet, in the palm of your hand. I would recommend the table to start with, however. Have the least illumination with which you can comfortably work. One low lamp, standing be-hind you so that it does not reflect in the crystal, is the ideal.

Sit for ten minutes or so in quiet reverie, without looking at the crystal. Try not to think of anything in particular, but to keep your mind a blank. Then gaze into the crystal. Look at its center point. Of course there is no real point there, but look into the center and keep your mind blank. Sit as still and as quietly as possible. You may remain that way for fifteen to twenty minutes with nothing happening. Do not be discouraged, and do not try for a longer period. Give it a rest and try the following, or next available night. It may well take a number of such sittings before you get results. Then one evening, as you sit staring into the crystal, you will realize that it is becoming cloudy. It is as though the small sphere were filling with steam or smoke. This will get thicker and thicker. Again you may get no more than this for a number of sittings. It may be, of course, that the very first time you try you will get the clouding over followed by the next stage—the unveiling.

The clouds in the ball will eventually seem to "roll back" from the center, and you will see a scene for all the world like a picture on a miniature television set. At first, and perhaps for some considerable period, you will have no control over what you see. It may be some-thing from the past, the present, or the future. What you see may, again, be open to interpretation. For ex-ample, I was once expecting some visitors from out of state. Looking in a crystal to see where, on their jour-ney, they might be I saw a scene of small boats on a stretch of water. It seemed to have no bearing whatso-ever on my expected visitors. Later, after their arrival, I checked to see where they were at the time I had been looking into the crystal. They said they had been crossing the Throgs Neck Bridge, on to Long Island, New York. The bridge, of course, crosses a stretch of water usually dotted with small boats!

With practice you can arrange to see what you want

to see. When sitting quietly, for the period immediately prior to scrying, concentrate on the person or thing you wish to see. Then, when you turn to the crystal, again clear your mind. The scene which will develop in the ball will deal with your preparatory thoughts.

If you cannot obtain a crystal, or even a glass ball, of suitable quality it is possible to use a regular convex magnifying lens. Polished carefully, and laid on the black velvet, it will work almost as well as the ball. Whichever you use, ball or lens, keep it purely for your scrying. Let no one else use it, or even handle it. Keep it wrapped in a cloth, or its velvet, and do not permit sunlight to strike it. Many seers say that to hold the crystal up to the light of a full moon will "charge" it. Before using it, if you wish, you may wash the ball in pure water, dry it, and then hold it cupped in your hands for a few moments to "warm" it.

A dark, or gazing mirror is often used in lieu of a crystal. You may recall, in Scott's *Waverley Novels,* the tale of My Aunt Margaret's mirror, in which the Paduan Doctor Baptisti Damiotti shows a distant scene to the ladies who were anxious about an absent husband. The mirror may be of any shape and is best if made by yourself. The method, according to an old book on the subject, is to procure a new piece of glass, free from flaws. Make it opaque by coating it three times with asphaltum. To make the asphalt stick to the glass, clean it well with turpentine. Lay on the asphalt with a camel hair brush. If you can obtain a piece of black plexiglass, completely free of scratches, that will make a usable mirror. The method of scrying with a mirror is the same as for the crystal.

Other objects are used—a glass of clear water, for instance. A blot of ink in the palm of the hand, as used by the Hindus. Precious stones are occasionally made use of, especially a pale green beryl. Witches will frequently use a highly polished disc of copper. Included in the frescoes around the walls of the Initiation Room, in the Villa of Mysteries at Pompeii, is a scene showing the Initiate gazing into a concave silver bowl, held by Silenus. Behind him a priest holds up a Dionysiac mask. Catching the reflection of the mask in the bowl would trigger the scenes of the life of Dionysus, so that the Initiate would re-live them. Once you have "got the knack" almost anything can be used. Basically scrying is just a form of self-hypnosis. Where it differs from straight-forward self-hypnosis is in frequently presenting scenes completely unknown to the practitioner—scenes which are definitely precognitive.

XXI

SÉANCE

The actual meaning of the word *séance* is "sitting." It is the sitting together of a group of people for an occult experiment. The group is usually of six to eight people. You sit with a professional medium or you can sit with some friends and a Ouija board. Both would be séances.

Séances are best held in the late evening. Theoretically there is no reason why they should not be held at any time—the middle of the morning or afternoon, for instance. In practice, however, the evening seems to bring an atmosphere much more favorable to success. There seems a certain stillness and clarity which is missing during the day. In addition, the later the evening the less chance of interruption from unexpected visitors. Darkness in itself helps the atmosphere and aids concentration. Do not try to work in complete darkness, but do have low lighting.

With physical mediums phenomena such as telekinesis (the moving of objects without physical contact), levitation and materialization (e.g. ectoplasm) may be experienced. Trumpets move about the room with voices coming from them. These trumpets are usually painted with luminous paint so that their movements can be followed. Musical instruments, such as guitars, banjos, accordions, tambourines, are played without human contact. Heavy objects become light enough to be raised by the touch of a finger, and light objects are suddenly so heavy they can hardly be lifted. Winds blow across the séance room, although all windows and doors are firmly closed. The sitters feel touches and taps on the arms, face and head.

With a trance medium psychical phenomena is experienced, which may include automatic writing but is usually speaking by or through the medium. Although frequently appearing quite normal the medium invariably is in a deep trance at the time of the manifestations. He (or she) may describe, in his own voice, people and things he can "see" or "hear" and speak for the deceased with his own voice. Or, in the case of "direct voice," may actually speak with the voice of the deceased. In the course of one sitting as many as twenty different voices may issue from a direct-voice medium's mouth, each quite different and instantly recognizable by the person present to whom it is directed.

Many mediums work in, or before, a "cabinet." This can be anything from a solid wooden construction, with a door or curtained front, to a piece of string across the corner of the room with a curtain draped over it. With physical mediums, if musical instruments are to be played they are usually placed inside the cabinet while the medium sits outside. The medium Eusapia Palladino would sit before a makeshift "cabinet" but for her the instruments did not necessarily have to be inside. Camille Flammarion describes ("Mysterious Psychic Forces") an interesting experiment: "I tried the experiment . . . by holding the accordion myself, and not letting it be touched by the medium . . . I take a little accordion, bought that evening in a bazaar, and, approaching the table and remaining in a standing position, I hold the accordion by one side resting two fingers upon the keys, in such a way as to permit the air to pass in case the instrument should begin to play.

"So held, it is vertically suspended by the stretching out of my right hand to the height of my head, and above the head of the medium. We make sure that her hands are all the time tightly held . . . After a short wait of five or six seconds I feel the accordion drawn by its free end; the bellows is immediately pushed in several times successively, and at the same time music is heard. There is not the least doubt that a hand, a pair of pincers, or what-not, has hold of the lower end of the instrument. I perceive very well the resistance of this prehensile organ. All possibility of fraud is eliminated. . . ."

When sitting with psychic mediums you must, as with all occult matters, try to keep an open mind, neither hostile nor gullible. If the medium tells you that there is "an elderly gentleman approaching. He has gray hair and walks forward with a happy smile and his arms outstretched towards you," do not say "Oh, that must be my father!" Say, rather, "Yes, please go on." In other words, do not feed information. Do not give your name to the medium before the sitting. Listen for small, intimate details, rather than generalities. If you can have someone with you, all to the good. In a group séance always appoint someone to take notes.

If you have a number of friends equally interested in exploring the supernatural it can be very worthwhile to organize yourselves into a society. What you call yourselves is really immaterial. It might be *The Blanksville Society of the Occult*, or something a little more pretentious like *The Parapsychology Society of Blanksville*. Arrange regular meetings; weekly, bi-weekly or monthly. Every sixth meeting or so should be a business one where you can plan what will be done at the other meetings. Perhaps a different séance each week: talking board one week; pendulum next week; ESP experiments next, and so on. Alternatively you may like to work on one aspect of the occult for a number of weeks before moving on to another. The results of the séance can also be discussed at the business meetings. You might even fix a small donation or membership fee, and use the money to have a professional medium visit the group, though great care should be exercised in choosing such a medium since there are a number of outright frauds in the field.

Do not let your séances run too long. It is so easy to get completely absorbed and find that several hours slipped by while working the talking board, or testing your possible ESP. Decide that the séance will run from, say, 8:00 P.M. till 11:00 P.M. Three hours should be ample. Let the Note-taker keep an eye on the time. Should you be in the middle of an exceptionally interesting item at the time the Note-taker points out the finishing time (and this will happen many times!) give yourselves another fifteen minutes and arrange with your "spirit contact" to carry on the "conversation" at the following week's séance. In this way you will avoid straining yourselves—or your "psychic power"—and will also get you off to a good start at the next sitting. Have fun!

XXII

SPIRIT PHOTOGRAPHY

On June 25th, 1909 a Supplement to the English *The Times' Weekly* published the following:

"The photographic world has once more had its attention drawn to the claims of what is called 'spirit' photography; and a committee has been formed, under the auspices of the *Daily Mail*, which has been investigating the subject. Three spiritualists and three expert photographers formed the committee. The three spiritualists reported that the photographers were not in a proper frame of mind to succeed in obtaining 'spirit' photographs. The photographers announced that no scrap of evidence was put before them to show that 'spirit' photography was possible. But they went further. . . . They invited the submission to them of 'spirit' photographs, and, having examined these critically, they report that not only did they not testify to their supernatural production, but that they bore on the faces of them circumstantial evidence of the way in which they had been produced; in other words, that the prints were not mysteries, but self-revealed 'fakes.' "

The reporter went on to explain how many of the fakes were produced, and the tell-tale signs that were on many prints. The most common method, in those days, involved the use of a secondary negative or positive. Photographic plates were bought by the investigators, and duly initialed to avoid any "switching" on the part of the photographer. They were then put into the slide, exposed, taken out and developed under strict supervision. But unknown to the investigators there was a prepared positive already inside the "dark-slide" of the camera into which they put the purchased, and initialed, plates. When the exposure was made it produced the "spirit" image. It remained there, undetected, on the removal of the plate.

Other so-called "spirits" were produced—and still are —in the developing stage of the photograph. And in the early days of photography there was a lot of innocent, or unconscious, fraud here. Due to poor developing, incorrect chemicals, and the like, finished portraits would appear with strange white shapes and streaks. The spiritualists hailed these as materializations invisible to the naked eye, which had been picked up by the camera. Amongst all this fraud, conscious and unconscious, there did appear one or two seemingly inexplicable spirit-photographs. These were, however, separate and individual instances. It was not until 1962 that there was to be any "spirit-photographer" who could produce repeatable phenomena of this type.

This king of present-day spirit-photography—or, more accurately, *thought*-photography—is Ted Serios. Keeping up with the times he uses a Polaroid Land camera to produce his pictures. Rather than photographs of "the dear departed" Serios produces an amazing assortment of "thought-forms" on the Polaroid print. He may think of a building, and there is a building—not just any building but the particular one he set out to get. His method of operation is seemingly, simplicity itself. Fresh film is loaded into the camera—anybody's camera. He points it at himself, or someone else; may point it at him. When he feels he is ready, he clicks the shutter, or signals someone else to click it. The picture is then ready to examine within seconds. Not every single shot is successful, of course; that is, perhaps, too much to expect. But an amazingly high percentage are incredibly accurate.

Ted Serios was first "recognized" by the Illinois Society for Psychic Research. Curtis Fuller was president of the society and to him should go credit for bringing this amazing man to the attention of the public. Unfortunately he does not get this credit. Nor does Dr. Jule Eisenbud, who spent over four years of time and countless dollars out of his own pocket, in thoroughly and completely investigating Ted Serios. Why do these two brilliant men not get their deserved credit? Probably for the same reason that so many scientific pioneers of the past went unrecognized in their early years. "Science" is notoriously conservative, almost to the point where it becomes a vicious circle of "I will believe it if I can see proof of it; but I will not look for proof of it until I believe it!" Curtis Fuller himself deals very well with the feelings, or non-feelings, of the "authorities" in his editorials to *Fate* magazine, August 1967 and December 1967.

To experiment with spirit, or thought, photography you need nothing more than a camera. In fact you do not even need that, as you will see. Experimenting the Serios way use a Polaroid Land camera. After deciding what to produce on film sit for a while thinking hard about it. Take something relatively simple. Either a very simple design or something with which you are extremely familiar. When you feel you have the object firmly in mind, point the camera directly at your face and loose the shutter. Do not try to "look into" the lens. If you do you will find you lose the concentration on the subject. Ted Serios uses what he terms a *gismo*. It is a means of channeling his concentrated thoughts into the camera lens; a funnel, if you like. Needless to say this gadget always excites suspicion of fraud. It has, of course, been thoroughly investigated. In fact other gismos have been made for Serios to use, without diminishing his results, by the investigators themselves. The plastic tube which holds the solution for coating Polaroid prints is frequently used. Cut off the end so that it is a simple cylinder. Cover both ends with cellophane, or scotch-tape, and blacken one of the ends with a felt-tipped pen. This gismo is then held against the lens as you point the camera at yourself.

If you do not have a Polaroid camera you can use a

camera of practically any other sort. The joy of a Polaroid is that you have results right away. With a regular camera you must wait patiently for your film to go away and be processed and then come back, before you find —perhaps nothing! Let us not fool ourselves, the possibilities of everybody getting Serios-quality results is infinitesimal—but the possibility *is* still there. The more people who try, the better chance of finding them.

There is an experiment which you can try, and stand every chance of success, that is remarkably simple to do and does not even call for use of a camera. It was carried out with great success in Los Angeles, in 1932, with a number of prominent scientists present and has since been repeated any number of times with similar results. In this early experiment the participants gathered in a photographic darkroom. The only light came from a photographic "safelight"—a light which, by virtue of its color, would not effect the emulsion of the sensitized photographic paper in any way. Two or three sheets of photographic paper were laid in different parts of the room so that there would be a record of any possible light leak.

Further sheets of paper were then cut into strips and given to the participants. They held these strips, by the ends, so that they curved around their foreheads, without actually touching the skin. The sensitized side of the paper was towards the skin. Each then concentrated hard on a particular object of his own choosing. After a while the papers were gathered up. The objects chosen were noted and the papers duly developed. It was found that the check-sheets, about the room, were blank; indicating no light leak of any sort present in the room. But the paper strips were quite different. On many of them had appeared images which were indisputably the very objects being thought by the experimenters—true thought-photographs.

A variation to the above might be to load your various strips, or even squares, into envelopes and seal them, in the darkroom. They could then be brought out into the light and passed out for concentration. This would save trying to squeeze a number of experimenters into one small darkroom. It might also be interesting to see what results, or what better results, would be obtained by having a number of people concentrating on one piece of paper. They would, of course, have to all think of the same object.

Other experiments will probably suggest themselves and should be tried. If you think you are getting too wild or "far out" just remember, ". . . almost all really new ideas have a certain aspect of foolishness when they are first produced."* If you are a keen photographer, or have one in your group, why not experiment with different types of film? For instance, put up a screen—try with a regular white screen and also try with a black screen—and have the experimenters concentrate their thought on that. Then photograph the screen. Try it, especially photographing with infra-red film. This is one experiment I have not yet tried myself, so I will be especially interested to hear from anyone who does try it. Do not forget to keep detailed notes of all you do. Note the light available; the film used; apertures; types of paper; number of people concentrating; proportions of male and female; positions; distances from screen/paper/film. Note every little detail. If you have success —and I do not guarantee it—you will then be in a posi-tion to repeat that success. And repetition can be all important.

*Alfred N. Whitehead.

149

XXIII

TALKING BOARD

The majority of people experience their first brush with the occult through the "talking board." Today there are two or three varieties on the market but the original, commercially-produced, board was the so-called "Ouija" (from the French *oui* and the German *ja*, both meaning "yes") of William Fuld. This is a smooth-surfaced, rectangular board with the letters of the alphabet written across it in two curving lines. Below the letters are the numbers one through nine, plus zero. Also on the board appear the words "YES," "NO," and "GOODBYE." With the board comes a sliding pointer, or *planchette,* which rests on three felt-covered feet and has a circular window through which the letters of the board may be read.

The *modus operandi* for the Ouija board is for two people to sit facing one another with the board between them, resting on their knees. The planchette, at the outset, sits in the center of the board and the participants each have their fingers resting lightly on it. By gliding about the board and stopping over different letters the planchette spells out messages and answers to questions put to it. It moves, seemingly, of its own volition. Many people believe that the board is actually controlled by the "spirits" of the dead, who are trying to converse with us. Whether or not this is so, to a person using the board for the first time the more obvious explanation is that the person sitting with him is pushing it. Let us look at a typical case:

Jim had been invited to his first talking board séance. He was sitting at the board opposite his hostess, Mrs.

Wilson. After a few moments, in answer to Mrs. Wilson's repeated question "Is there any spirit present?" the planchette started to slide across the board to the word *YES*. It was quite a firm movement. So firm, in fact, that Jim had no doubt at all that Mrs. Wilson herself was responsible for it.

"Do you have a message for any person here?" asked Mrs. Wilson.

YES repeated the board, then proceeded to slide around to point directly at *J, I* and *M—Jim!* Jim, however, remained unimpressed. So he remained until the planchette, continuing on its way, spelled out the message: *LOOK ONE MORE TIME BUTCH*. Suddenly he became very much interested. "Butch" was the nickname of a favorite uncle who had recently died. Mrs. Wilson knew nothing of either the nickname or even the uncle. Added to that the rest of the message made a great deal of sense to him. After his uncle had died Jim had spent many hours going through his effects looking for a particular book which Uncle Butch had always been meaning to give him. He had been unable to find it and had virtually given up the search. *Look one more time* then made a great deal of sense and was again something of which Mrs. Wilson was ignorant.

Can we now, then, assume that the message came from the spirit of Jim's dead Uncle Butch? The answer is no, for although the message "clears" Mrs. Wilson of pushing it does not clear the other participant—Jim himself. Obviously Jim was not *consciously* pushing the planchette, but he may well have been doing so *unconsciously*. At the back of his mind he may still have been thinking of his search for the book. He may even have been half hoping that Uncle Butch *would* come and tell him where it was (and here would have been the only point in favor of supernatural contact—if Jim had received a message telling him of the actual location of the missing item). So long as the information obtained from the board was known to any person present then there can be no definite proof of contact with any type of "spirit" world. Indeed, even if no person actually in the room knew the information obtained there might still be another explanation rather than the spirit one. For, as will be realized from the article on Extra-Sensory Perception, Jim or Mrs. Wilson could conceivably "pick up" information from a person or persons not even present in the room.

Does all this mean that there is definitely nothing worthwhile to be obtained from the talking board? Not at all, for information has been received on a number of occasions which, on the face of it, was unknown to any living person. We shall see that a great deal of interesting research can be done with a board, a lot of fun may be had and, if nothing else, the existence of ESP can be established to your own satisfaction.

What actually causes the planchette to move? Almost certainly it is the muscle power of the participants. That they are not pushing it consciously we have seen, yet for it to move at all they must have their fingers on it—ergo, they must be responsible for the movement. The question, then, is what *directs* the movement? Who or what decides on the answers or messages? This you must decide for yourself after due experimentation. If you already have a board then you can start to experiment right away in the manner to be suggested.

There are, however, at least two faults in the design of the Ouija board (in the author's opinion) that might be mentioned here. One is but a slight inconvenience; the fact that when the planchette goes to the extremities of the board one foot of the planchette may slip over the edge and before continuing you must lift it back on. The other fault, however, is more serious, and is in the design of the planchette. The instructions given say: "the mysterious message indicator (planchette) will commence to move . . . As it passes over Ouija talking board each letter of a message is received as it appears through the transparent window covered by the message indicator." This is not strictly true. Sometimes you may receive a string of letters that seem to make no sense whatsoever—until it is realized that the planchette is no longer showing the relevant letters through its plastic "window" on the one line, but is pointing with its tapered end to the letters on the line above. Consequently one must always watch and note two sets of letters all the time!

The indication that only two people may use the board at any one time is also quite incorrect. The board should be placed in the center of a small table and may be used by as many people as can squeeze around it. A suggested "working group" for the Ouija board is four people. For the home-made one, shortly to be described, six to eight people make a good group. It is preferable that there should be equal numbers of each sex around it, seated alternately. (Male and female, in this and other psychic experiments, seem to act in a way analogous to the positive and negative terminals of a battery.) It is a good idea to always include an extra person to take notes. Record keeping is one of the most important parts of any form of psychic research. The human memory is notoriously unreliable so do not think that you can just write down everything that happened *after* the experiment. Play safe and note it as it happens. An additional safeguard might even be to have a tape-recorder running throughout, in case the note-taker should miss something.

For those who do not own one or other of the commercially produced boards an equally effective set-up may be produced using lettered pieces of paper and a wine-glass! Choose a small table with a smooth surface; no cracks or joins. Turn a wine glass upside down on it and see that it will slide about quite freely. Now, write the letters of the alphabet boldly on individual squares of paper. The paper should be about one-and-a-half inches square. The letters should be distinct, preferably capitals. Also, on squares of paper, write the numbers one through nine and zero, and the words "YES" "NO" "GOODBYE" and "REPHRASE." Now arrange the paper squares in a circle around the edge of the table, facing inwards. It should be one continuous circle with the numbers following on from the letters and the "YES" and "NO" inserted at opposite poles top and bottom, and "GOODBYE" and "REPHRASE" opposite each other at the sides. (See Fig. 6.)

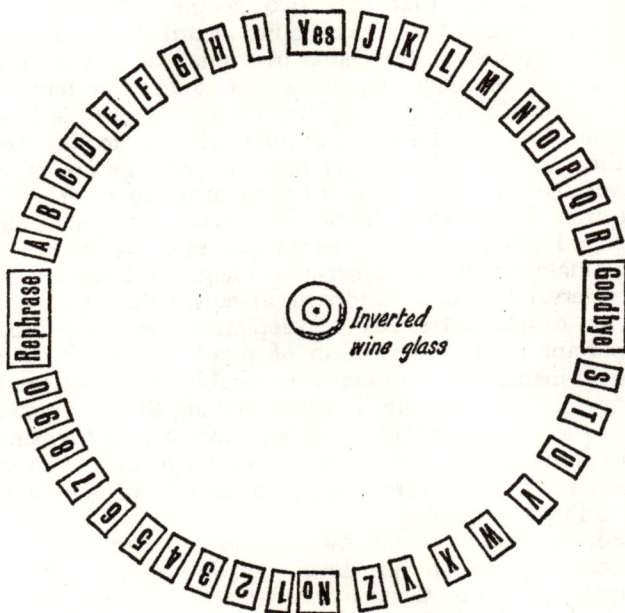

Fig. 6

Each person around the table places a finger lightly on the edge of the wine-glass. If you have six to eight people present have only four of them work the glass at one time. Every half hour or so change the "workers." This will help verify that no one person is pushing. For greater effect the finger rested on the glass should be

154

the middle finger of the working hand (right hand for right-handed people; left hand for left-handed people).

One person, and *one person only*, should be elected Spokesman. If anyone else has a question they must give it to the Spokesman to ask. Different people asking different questions, often at the same time, can lead to confusion even in ordinary life! It is permissible to change Spokesman at intervals—perhaps desirable to do so, to find out who seems to get the best results—so long as the change-over is complete and definite.

It is a good idea to prepare a list of questions before the sitting. This way there will be no long pause while everyone racks his brains to think of something to ask. It also, of course, helps the Note-taker if all he or she has to do is fill in the answers and the messages. Inevitably the newcomer to the talking board will want to ask such questions as "When will I die?" "When will I marry?" "Who will I marry?" (young ladies especially want to know the last two!), etc. Get these questions out of your system by all means. But then let's get down to some more serious investigating.

Sit around the table and talk for a while before starting. Perhaps have a drink, or a snack. The aim is to get relaxed. Low lighting is certainly not essential for the sitting but there can be no question that it does seem to help create the right atmosphere. Don't go to the lengths of having just one, low-watt, red bulb, so that everyone is straining their eyes! What is termed "television lighting" would seem ideal. When ready lay out the paper and the glass; put your fingers on the glass, and from then on the Spokesman is in charge. He starts by asking, in a normal voice, "Is there anybody there, please?" The question may be repeated from time to time until it will be noticed that the glass is sliding, very gradually, across the table to the word *YES*. When it arrives there the Spokesman will say "Thank you. Will you please return to the center?" and the glass will do so. For this initial movement it may be necessary to wait anything from two to twenty minutes, depend-

155

ing on the "power" (for want of a better word) of the people present. In the same way the glass may move very slowly for the first few questions, or it may start straight off with a firm, definite action.

At no time should anyone present attempt to PUSH the glass. This is most important. Certainly it would be easy to push it without anyone knowing, and have a few laughs at the expense of your friends—but what is the point? If you are planning a talking board séance for goodness sake omit anyone whom you feel may not take it seriously; otherwise everything will be pointless and those who are serious will have a wasted evening. This does not mean that you must sit straight-faced all evening! Far from it; much fun may be had. What it boils down to is, *do not push* the glass or planchette and do not ask stupid, pointless questions. Initially everyone taking part will feel sure, in his or her own mind, that someone present *is* pushing. This is a natural suspicion. Bear with it for a while; you will soon find it allayed.

After establishing contact the sitting may proceed on lines such as the following:

"Is there anyone there, please?"
YES
"Are you willing to speak with us?"
YES
"Do you have a message for anyone here?"
YES
"Would you please give the name or the initials of the person?"
J. B. D.
"Is the message for John?"
YES
"Would you please spell out the message?"
WAIT FOR THE SMUMRF
"Would you repeat the last word, please?"
SUMMER
"Thank you. Carry on with the message."

NOW IS TOSOON
"Do you mean 'Now is too soon?'"
YES
"Is there more to the message?"
NO

It will be seen that occasionally the letters of a word are slightly jumbled. If there is any doubt about anything simply ask for a repeat. In the above example, where the phrase *Wait for the smumrf* appears, not only are the letters of the last word jumbled but there is an "f" given instead of an "e." It could have been that the glass, in error, moved to the letter next to the one it meant. It could also have been that it stopped half way between the two letters and the note-taker assumed it was the one rather than the other. Should it ever happen that it does point between two letters the Spokesman has only to say, "Please point exactly to the letter you mean," or "Is that an *E* or an *F*?" and the planchette will straighten up. The Spokesman should speak to it quite naturally, as if talking to another person.

You will find that your questions must be very precise. With the Ouija board it is occasionally found that the planchette refuses to move in answer to a question. If the questioner had stopped to think he may have realized that the question was ambiguous—the poor board did not know which of two or more answers was wanted! On the home-made layout described above we have allowed for such an occurrence by including the word "REPHRASE." Should the Spokesman ever inadvertently ask a question that could be taken more than one way you will find the glass will slide across to "REPHRASE," and he can then put the question in a more precise manner. Even so the glass will once in a while refuse to answer a question. This is usually when you are inquiring a little too closely about the future. It seems there are some things which we are just not supposed to know.

When a long message is being spelled out it is often

easier to understand it if the glass is asked to stop briefly in the center of the table to signify the end of each word. If ever the movement seems sluggish a useful, and very amusing, way to get the glass moving faster is for the Spokesman to ask it to move round and round the circle, getting faster and faster. The glass will respond by eventually moving so fast that it will be almost impossible to keep your fingers on it!

If questions of a serious nature are prepared much interesting information may be gathered. A few suggested questions are given below. Think up others of your own. Follow up on answers that seem particularly promising.

Sample questions:

Did you once live on Earth?
What was your name in that life?
In what country did you live?
What year did you die?
What was your occupation?
Where is your body buried?
Were you married?
Is your wife still alive?
Did you have any children?
Are any of your descendants alive?
Where are they living?
Are you related to anyone here, at this table?
Can you "materialize" in any way?
Where you are, are there "spirits" from places other than Earth?
Are there "evil" spirits?
If so, why are they evil?
Will they always be evil?
What does one experience at the moment of death?

From the above it may well be possible to follow up the séance by checking out some of the answers received. This is what can really make a sitting interesting. Did the "spirit" really live at the time claimed? Can his grave be found? Check burial grounds, church records, public records, anything that might help. Check a copy of the local newspaper of the time of both his birth and death, to see if there was any notice of the event. Was the "spirit" ever in the army? If so check army records.

But suppose the answer to the first question "Did you once live on Earth?" happens to be *NO?* Where do we go from there? Well, there are still a number of fascinating questions to ask, though unfortunately there will be few answers that you will be able to verify. Here are a few suggested questions:

Have you ever lived on another planet?
Is there life, as we know it, on any other planet?
Are you going to be born on this Earth sometime in
the future?
Can you communicate with the "spirits" of people
who *have* lived on Earth?
Where are you?
Of what type of matter are you made?
Do you have emotions?
Do you know fear?
If so, fear of what?
Do you have any sense of time, as we know it?

If you have a sufficient number of people interested in the talking board to form two groups it is sometimes possible to experiment in what is known as "cross-correspondence." This can become very complicated but need not be initially. Let us call our two groups A and B. Then let us appoint an unbiased Coordinator named X. During their initial sittings groups A and B will tell their respective "spirits" what they wish to do. It can be explained like this:

SPOKESMAN: "We want to do a cross-correspondence with our other group. They are meeting at John's house, 1144 East Main Street, tomorrow night at nine o'clock. During our sitting here tonight please start a message that you will continue with them."

Then somewhere in the material that each group receives will be *part* of a message. On the face of it there may be nothing unusual. It may blend in with whatever else is received. But each group will send the record of its sitting to X. He should be an intelligent, fairly learned person. His job it is to search through both sets of material and find the total message. An example may help give the picture. Let us suppose that among the many pages of Group A's material X finds this:

GROUP A   *Spokesman*: "What sort of place are you in now?" IT IS VERY PLEAS-ANT, AS THOUGH THE WINTER IS PAST, THE RAIN IS OVER AND GONE AND EVERYTHING IS NICE AND FRESH AGAIN—ALMOST A REBIRTH.

Something suddenly strikes X as sounding vaguely familiar. He very carefully goes through Group B's equally lengthy material. He finally comes across the passage:

GROUP B   *Spokesman*: "Is there anything you knew on Earth that you miss?"
NO
"Can everything be experienced where you are, then?"
YES

"The different seasons?"
OH YES. EVEN WHEN THE
FLOWERS APPEAR ON THE
EARTH, THE TIME OF THE
SINGING OF BIRDS, GAM-
BOLING OF LAMBS — EV-
ERYTHING REALLY.

Now X recognizes the whole phrase. It is a quotation from *The Song of Solomon* (ii.11,12): "For lo, the winter is past, the rain is over and gone; the flowers appear on the earth; the time of the singing of birds is come, and the voice of the turtle is heard in our land."

Such a cross-correspondence could be continued for a number of sessions. The main point with such an experiment is that neither group should see the other's notes and neither, of course, know what quotation to expect. If the Coordinator selects a quotation himself before-hand, and the Spokesmen ask that the continuing message "be the one being thought of by Mr. X," then it makes X's job a lot easier when it comes to searching for the quotation. However, in this case no more would be proved than the possibility of ESP between someone in each of the groups and X. To have the quotation, message, or whatever, known to *no one* beforehand is far more convincing—if tougher for X!

At the end of the sitting it is only polite to wish the "spirit" goodnight. The glass will go at once to the "GOODNIGHT" in the circle of letters. Before closing, if the sitting has seemed especially successful, there is no reason why you should not make a date to meet with the same "spirit" at your next sitting, to con-tinue where you left off.

If in checking out information received from the board you draw a blank, do not be too disappointed. It has been said that as much as 80% of what you receive is really worthless. But the other 20% more than makes up for it. And sifting the worthwhile from the worthless can be really fascinating!

XXIV

TABLE TIPPING

Table tipping is another product of the early days of Spiritualism. It is a form of psychic phenomena where a table is made to turn, tip and lift, by the mere con-tact of the sitters' fingers.

Start off with a small, light, table. Later on you will be able to achieve the same results with a larger, heavier one but initially use something about the size of a card table. However many persons are participating should sit evenly spaced around the table with their hands resting lightly on it. The hands should be close to the edge, palms down, and with the thumbs and outer fingers touching; forming a circle. As with the talking board a Spokesman should be elected who will do all the talking for the group. The Spokesman may be changed at intervals to give everyone a chance, so long as the change-over is a definite one.

The right kind of atmosphere is established by sitting at the table socially for a while; talking generally. Then the Spokesman takes command and asks, in a normal, clear voice, "Is there anyone there, please?"

He will repeat the question from time to time, and then add, "Please tip the table twice for *yes*."

It will soon be noticed that there is a slight movement from the table. It may be accompanied by odd creaking noises until, eventually, it will be found that the table has tipped slightly so that it is resting on only two of its legs. It will then fall back on to all four. The Spokesman should then repeat, "Is there anyone there, please? Tip the table twice for YES and three times for NO. Is there anyone there?"

To which the table should reply by twice tipping up

on its two legs and then falling back on to all four. Once contact has been established then you may proceed very much as with the talking board. If questions are kept to the YES-NO answer variety then the table will almost certainly be rocking merrily backwards and forwards all evening. If you want to go further and get specific messages then these can be spelled out by having the table tip once for A, twice for B, three times for C, etc., etc. At first this will seem a lengthy process but you will soon get used to it and laughingly find everyone counting the "thumps" together as the table rocks back to the floor.

The information obtained from the table may surprise you. Try not to take it too seriously however. Some of the material will be worthwhile, and its aquisition unexplainable certainly, but the vast majority will be virtually worthless—either facts drawn from your own unconscious mind, or outright fiction invented purely for your entertainment. For the serious investigator a set of leading questions, prepared beforehand, will be a boon. Questions, the answers to which can be checked and double-checked after the séance is over.

If you run out of questions, or you would like a change of pace or a short break, then a lot of fun may be had by "spinning" the table, and "walking" it. First of all, push back your chairs! The table can really become active so start by standing, or kneeling, at it rather than sitting. The Spokesman says, "Would you please go up to only one leg and see how fast you can spin around?"

The table will again go over on two legs and then, with a few words of encouragement, tip up on to one leg only. Now get ready to move! The table will start to rotate on its leg and you must move—in fact run—around to keep your hands on it. It will frequently turn so fast that you will just not be able to maintain the contact and may even end up tripping over one another and tumbling, with the table, to the floor.

A similar procedure will induce the table to walk about the room—tipping up and swinging from one leg to the other—while you trot along beside it. I have seen a table swing itself up on to a settee and have had reports of another which "climbed on to the pinao and, if it hadn't broken its leg, I'm sure would have given us a tune!"

The next step with the table would seem to be an attempt at complete levitation. On the face of it success would seem unlikely. Records of levitation, under test conditions, are few and far between—but it *has* been done. So why not give it a try? I quote briefly from one of the best known, and most carefully controlled, cases (that of a sitting with the medium Eusapia Palladino) in the chapter on *Mediums.* Although, in this instance, the levitation was done by an experienced, extremely developed, physical medium, she was working in a strange hotel room. She had an assortment of "men of science" around her, who were there specifically to test her alleged powers. One or two of them were almost certainly skeptical of these powers. These are harsh conditions for a medium, however experienced she may be. I see no reason, then, why others should not have the same success although they lack experience, for first of all they possess the all important "atmosphere." Sitting with friends, completely relaxed, and "at home," cannot help but draw out any latent powers you may have.

All in all the "conditions of power" ratios may well equal out. Certainly nothing is to be lost in trying. So go ahead . . . and let me know how you make out.

XXV

THE TAROT

Cartomancy is divination by cards. The oldest known cards used for this divination is the deck of Tarot, or *tarocchi*, cards. Their exact origin is unknown. Mathers, Etteilla, Lévi and others liked to think that they dated back to the ancient Egyptians; Chatto believed that they were invented by the Chinese. But there is little or no evidence for either of these theories. The most popular theory is that they were brought into Europe by the Gypsies, though even here their exact origin remains vague. The earliest known deck dates from the fourteenth century. De Givry claims there is a trace of the tarot in Germany as early as 1329, but does not enlarge on it.

The deck itself consists of seventy-eight cards in two parts. These parts are called the Minor Arcana and the Major Arcana. The Minor Arcana is made up of fifty-six of the cards, divided, again, into four suits of four-teen cards each. It is from this Minor Arcana of the Tarot that our everyday playing cards stem. The suits are Swords, Pentacles (sometimes called Coins), Wands (sometimes called Staves), and Cups. Their modern counterparts are Spades, Diamonds, Clubs, and Hearts respectively. Each suit numbers one (or Ace) through ten with a Page, Knight, Queen and King. At some stage in their development the Knight dropped out and the Page became known as the Jack, or Knave.

The Major Arcana, otherwise known as the Trumps Major, has twenty-two cards, each an allegorical figure of complicated symbolic meaning. These figures are, by many occultists, attributed to the twenty-two letters of the Hebrew alphabet. Thus:

1 The Magician (or Juggler)	Aleph
2 The High Priestess	Beth
3 The Empress	Gimel
4 The Emperor	Daleth
5 The Hierophant	Heh
6 The Lovers	Vav
7 The Chariot	Zain
8 Justice	Cheth
9 The Hermit	Teth
10 The Wheel of Fortune	Yod
11 Strength	Kaph
12 The Hanged Man	Lamed
13 Death	Mem
14 Temperance	Nun
15 The Devil	Samekh
16 The Tower	Ayin
17 The Star	Peh
18 The Moon	Tzaddi
19 The Sun	Qoph
20 Judgment	Resh
21 The World	Shin
0 The Fool	Tav

Unfortunately the occultists cannot agree, even on this, for while MacGregor Mathers, for instance, attributes the cards as I have shown, Paul F. Case puts The Fool at the beginning. This moves them all up one, and gives:

0 The Fool	Aleph
1 The Magician	Beth
2 The High Priestess	Gimel
etc.	

To further complicate the issue A. E. Waite and Paul Case give the number 8 to Strength and 11 to Justice while virtually every other writer, and deck, shows 8 to be Justice and 11 Strength!

Many writers on the tarot frighten away would-be students with their needlessly veiled and lofty descriptions and interpretations. One such writer says, of the Major Arcana, "Their symbolism is a type of shorthand for metaphysics and mysticism. Here are truths of so subtle and divine an order that to express them badly in human language would be a sacrilege. Only esoteric symbolism can reveal them to the inner spirit of the seeker." He does, however, go on to express them in human language—and I must confess that in this chapter I aim to do the same. What does the man-in-the-street care for revelations to his inner spirit by esoteric symbolism? He has a deck of tarot cards and wants to learn to divine for his friends. So I will here leave the deeper meanings—and I do not deny that they exist—to the researchers, and pass on to the "how-to" part of this article.

There are a number of methods of divining with the tarot but the most straightforward, especially for the beginner, is the Ancient Celtic method. You first take from the deck the card you feel most representative of the person for whom you are reading. To start with you should use the traditional card for this. If your subject has dark hair and eyes the card (called the *Significator*) should be from the Swords suit. For fair hair and blue eyes, from the Wands suit. For black hair and dark eyes, from the Pentacles suit. And for light brown hair and gray, blue or hazel eyes, from the Cups suit. Of these suits, if the person is an older man use the King of the suit. If a younger man, the Knight; a youth, the Page. If an older woman, use the Queen. If a younger woman, the Page.

Later on, when you are much more familiar with the cards, it will be better to study the person for whom you are reading and then to go carefully through *all* the cards looking for the Significator. There will be perhaps three or four that somehow strike you as being *his,* or *her,* cards. They may not necessarily depict a single character. They might even show a scene (e.g. 18–The Moon). Studying these three or four further you will finally decide on just one card as, more than the others, being *the* one. It is difficult to describe just how you know the card. It is a feeling; a sensation. This card is the true Significator.

Pass the remainder of the cards to the subject and ask him to shuffle them a number of times. When he has done this ask him to spread them all out face down. He is then to pick out any ten cards and pass them, in a pile, to you. The other cards may then be placed on one side, for you only use these ten together with the Significator in the Ancient Celtic method.

The Significator is laid down, face upwards, in the center. This card shows, or indicates, the "front" that the subject puts up. It shows the type of impression that he likes other people to have of him. This is then covered by the first card the subject picked, laid face downwards. This is known as "what covers him." Crosswise, on these two cards, is placed the second one he picked. This is what crosses him. The third card is placed above—what crowns him—and the fourth card below—what is beneath him. To the right goes the fifth card—what is behind him. To the left goes the sixth—what is before him. The remaining four cards are placed in order over on the far right, one above the other; seventh, eighth, ninth, and tenth. These are: Himself, His House, His Hopes and Fears, and What Will Come, respectively. (See figure 7.)

The cards are then turned over one at a time as you give the individual interpretations—which will be dealt with below—each being looked at in its particular position. In the case of giving a general reading, card number one—what covers him—shows the general atmosphere around the subject; the influences at work. (If you are divining to answer a specific question for the subject, in which case he should have concentrated on the question as he shuffled them and picked the ten cards, then this first card shows the influence at work around the question.)

The second card shows what forces and influences are working against him. It may even show, or indicate, an actual person who is hindering, or "crossing" him, in some way. Card number three, what crowns him, shows his ideals—what he is really aiming for—although he may not finally get there. Number four, beneath him, shows the real him; the unconscious self—the actual basis of him. Number five, behind him, shows what has already taken place. It could be either the immediate past or it could show, in general terms, his whole past life. Number six, on the other hand, shows what is immediately coming into effect.

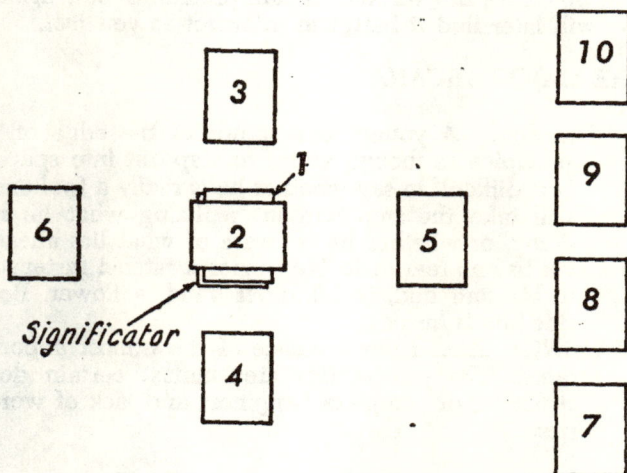

Fig. 7

Starting up the final four cards, number seven shows more of the subject himself, how he will fare generally in life and especially in the immediate future. Number eight is his house, his family and close friends. Number nine is his hopes and fears. Number ten is what will be the final outcome for him. It can be seen that some cards will confirm others. There should be similarities, for instance, between cards four and seven; similarities in three and nine. The whole should give some indication of what to expect from number ten. Should the majority of the cards be from the Major Arcana then you can be sure that the forces involved are powerful ones. Any changes will be fairly drastic changes; any set-backs will be severe set-backs; any advancements will be very major advancements.

Let us look now at the interpretations of the cards themselves. They must, of course, be interpreted in relation to the positions they occupy in the layout. I will give you here the traditional interpretations but, again, you will later find it better to interpret as you *feel*.

THE MAJOR ARCANA

0: *The Fool.* A young man stands at the edge of a precipice as though about to step out into space. It is difficult to say whether he is really a fool and will take the step without realizing what he is doing, or whether he is aware of what lies ahead yet has no fear of it. He carries a satchel fastened to his staff and, in his other hand, a flower. Beside him is his dog.

MEANING: Ahead lies a choice of the utmost importance. The possibilities are: almost certain destruction, or complete happiness and lack of worries.

1: *The Magician.* He is young; yet wise. He has confidence in his powers. He stands, in a garden, behind his table which holds the symbols of the

170

four suits of the Minor Arcana. In his hand he holds a wand or scepter (in some decks, a cup); about his waist coils a serpent. He might well be ageless.

MEANING: A position of authority is, or will be, held; the ability to direct power to where it will do the most good. Psychic power is possessed and could be greatly developed. Diplomacy is a trait.

2: *The High Priestess.* In some decks she appears as a female Pope, to judge from the high, tiered, miter. In others she wears the horns of Isis; between them the solar disc. At her feet may lie a crescent moon. There is a curtain, or tapestry, which hangs behind her, and on her knee rests a (sacred?) book. She may sit between the two pillars—the black pillar Boaz and the white pillar Jakin.

MEANING: Knowledge; ability to learn and to teach; serenity. She may represent unnoticed "power behind the throne," may indicate hidden influences working; secrets to be revealed later.

3: *The Empress.* A matronly woman sits on a throne with a scepter in her hand. There is a shield, or coat-of-arms, beside her. She wears a crown and is dressed in fine robes. Her throne stands in a garden.

MEANING: Marriage and the ruler of the house. Fine living—all the necessities plus the luxuries. Experience; understanding. Fruitfulness. The mother, or motherhood. Materially rather than physically inclined.

4: *The Emperor.* An elderly man in royal robes who sits on, or (in other decks) leans against, a throne. He wears a crown and holds a scepter and also an orb. He may have his shield leaning against his throne. He and his throne are out in the open, not far from the mountains.

MEANING: Leadership and ability to govern. Authority and knowledge. Protection and stability. Careful thought rather than sudden action.

5: *The Hierophant.* Sometimes called The Pope, for he wears the triple crown and holds, in his left hand, a staff with a triple cross at its head. His throne is placed between two pillars and before him are two priestly figures. In some decks he appears old and bearded, in others young and somewhat effeminate.

MEANING: Conservatism. Preference for the established method and order. Religiously inclined. Feeling the need to be approved, socially. Wishing to conform. A liking for a certain amount of authority but only when a scapegoat is available should things go awry.

6: *The Lovers.* They meet, in the sunshine, with a divine being watching over them. In some decks they are naked, in others clothed. Some decks also show a man between two women, rather than the one man and one woman.

MEANING: A coming together; uniting. Problems finally overcome. The start of a new, and promising project. In the deck with the three human figures: a choice between equally worthy objects. A possible struggle but promise of eventual great happiness.

7: *The Chariot.* A princely figure riding in a two-wheeled chariot drawn by two horses or two sphinxes. The chariot has a canopy supported by four pillars. The figure wears a crown and holds a scepter in his right hand.

MEANING: Triumph over obstacles. Conquest. Also

172

signifies arrival of help, or advice, at the hour of need. Can mean revenge.

8: *Justice.* (Waite and Gray show this as number 11, and *Strength* as number 8. The majority, and the older decks, show as I have shown here.) A figure, possibly female, sits between two pillars. Behind hangs a cloth or tapestry. The figure wears a crown and holds an upright sword in the right hand, a pair of scales in the left.

MEANING: As the title suggests, justness; fairness. Ability to judge and to make fair rules and laws. A balanced personality; a well balanced mind. Impartial and not easily swayed.

9: *The Hermit.* An old, bearded man in hooded robes. He carries a lantern in his right hand and leans on a staff.

MEANING: Wisdom. Learning through experience, rather than book-learning. A seeker. An escapist; an introvert. May also mean fraud and deceit. Also signifies the possibility of an unexpected journey.

10: *The Wheel of Fortune.* In some decks an actual wheel is depicted, between two uprights. To it are bound two animals; one ascending, the other descending. Above it is an angel or a sphinx. Other decks show a disc in the sky, bearing symbols and letters. A sphinx sits on the top of it and below, as though bound to it, is an Anubis-like figure—a jackal-headed man. At the corners of the card are figures: a bird, a lion, a bull, and a human.

MEANING: Good luck. Increase in fortune. Unexpected turn of events. Success.

11: *Strength.* (See note for number 8—*Justice*) A well-dressed woman, sometimes shown crowned, calmly closes the mouth of a ferocious lion. In some decks it could well be, from the position of her hands, that she is actually trying to *open* the lion's mouth. Either way she is obviously causing the lion to act contrary to his own wishes.

MEANING: Fortitude. Ability to endure hardship. Moral strength. Ability to forgive others their weaknesses and their hate. Loyalty.

12: *The Hanged Man.* A man hangs upside-down from a gibbet, by one foot. His other foot is bent so that it is crossed behind the hanging foot. His hands are held (or tied?) behind his back. He does not look particularly unhappy.

MEANING: Self-sacrifice. Generally meaning a willingness to let others go forward by yourself stepping back, *but* can also mean masochistic tendencies.

13: *Death.* A skeletal figure who reaps, with a scythe, a harvest of heads, hands and feet. In other decks the figure is dressed in black armor and rides a white horse. Beside him lies a fallen king.

MEANING: Inevitability. Uselessness of trying to change plans, or avoid a situation. May also mean sudden collapse when least expected.

14: *Temperance.* A winged figure pours liquid from one vessel to another. On the forehead of the figure is seen the solar disc. In some decks the figure stands with one foot in a stream, which flows down from mountains in the background. Over the mountains a great crown is barely discernible in the sky.

MEANING: Ability to coordinate. Diplomacy. Tact. A uniting. Impartiality.

15: *The Devil.* A great horned, bat-winged, figure stands, or crouches, protectively over two figures.

The figures are male and female and are attached to the rock, pillar, or altar on which the main figure stands, by ropes or chains about their necks. The figure is Pan-like in some decks, yet quite beneficent in appearance in others.

MEANING: Authority being removed and given to another. Seeming disaster which actually benefits others. Willing bondage. Enrollment.

16: *The Tower.* Sometimes called the *House of God* this card depicts a tower being struck by lightning. The top of the tower, shaped like a crown, topples and two figures fall to the ground. Sparks and debris fall on either side.

MEANING: Sudden, unexpected, change. Complete turnabout of views; way of life. Disruption. Bankruptcy; loss.

17: *The Star.* A large, eight-pointed star shines, with seven smaller stars, over a naked female who kneels at a stream. She is emptying two pitchers of water into the stream. A bird is alighting on a tree behind her.

MEANING: Change for the better. Clearing out the bad old for the good new. Hope and inspiration. Great promise for the future.

18: *The Moon.* The Moon, in both its full and its crescent forms, looks down upon two dog-like figures which bay up at it. Before the dogs is a pool or stream in which lies a lobster, crab, or crayfish. Behind the dogs rise two towers; one on either side.

MEANING: Intuition. Latent psychic power. Astral journeys. May also mean unforeseen perils and deception.

19: *The Sun.* A bright, full sun shines down upon two children standing together. Behind the children is a wall. In some decks there is only one child, seated on a horse. Over the wall behind the child are seen large sunflowers.

MEANING: Happiness and contentment. Achievement. Success and honors. The start of a new career. Freedom. A birth—either of a child, an idea, or a project.

20: *Judgment.* A divine being, holding a bannered trumpet to its lips, looks down on naked men and women standing in what appear to be coffins. In some decks the people clasp their hands together, in others they have them raised towards the trumpeter.

MEANING: A new life. Rejuvenation. A fresh start. Announcement of importance, affecting your progress. An introduction.

21: *The World.* A naked female holds a scepter in each hand. She has a flowing scarf flung over one shoulder. She is encircled by a wreath. In the four corners are the heads of a bird, a lion, an ox, and a man; similar to the figures around number 10—*The Wheel of Fortune.*

MEANING: Completion of a cycle. Attainment. Recognition. Reward. Acclaim. Graduation.

These then, are the twenty-two cards of the Major Arcana. The Minor Arcana I will not describe in as great detail because in many decks there are no scenes depicted; there is merely the number of suit emblems displayed. Because of this I would recommend that the beginner start with such a deck as the Pamela Colman Smith-Arthur E. Waite deck, for this gives a full scene to every card. In this way you can the sooner replace—or enlarge upon—the traditional meanings with your own interpretation of, and your own feelings about, the actual scene.

Of the four suits of the Minor Arcana, Wands is usually associated with Glory and Enterprise and the element of Fire. Swords is associated with Troubles and Misfortunes; the element is Air. Cups suit is Love and Happiness; the element, Water. Pentacles suit is Money. The element, Earth.

Wands Suit.

ACE OF WANDS: Beginning. Invention. Source. Inheritance.

TWO OF WANDS: Fortune. Riches. Opulence. Ownership.

THREE OF WANDS: Business success. Trade. Negotiation.

FOUR OF WANDS: Happy family life. Harmony. Social activities.

FIVE OF WANDS: Competition. Struggle. Hardship for limited time. Barter.

SIX OF WANDS: Conquest. Recognition. Triumph. Preparation for battle.

SEVEN OF WANDS: Uncertainty. Gradual success. Slow advancement.

EIGHT OF WANDS: Travel. Time for planning; observation. Preparedness.

NINE OF WANDS: Imminent travel. Possible troubles. Prepare for the worst.

TEN OF WANDS: Overcoming problem. Sweeping away opposition. Assertion.

PAGE OF WANDS: News—probably good. A message. A contract likely to be favorable.

KNIGHT OF WANDS: Separation. Departure. Flight. Re-location.

QUEEN OF WANDS: Woman of the house. Domesticity. Avarice.

KING OF WANDS: Family man. Inheritance. Honesty. Tolerance.

Swords Suit.

ACE OF SWORDS: Extremities of feelings. Fertility. Conquest. Activity.

TWO OF SWORDS: Indecision. Stalemate. Friendship. Impartiality.

THREE OF SWORDS: Sorrow. Quarrel. Infidelity. Love triangle.

FOUR OF SWORDS: Respite. Recuperation. Convalescence. Bad dreams.

FIVE OF SWORDS: Victory over odds. Success. Avertion of danger. Hidden danger.

SIX OF SWORDS: Escape. Reprieve. Journey through difficulties. Unknown destination.

SEVEN OF SWORDS: Overconfidence. Bluff. Unstable business.

EIGHT OF SWORDS: Self-criticism. Uncertainty. Sickness. Losses.

NINE OF SWORDS: Doubt. Fear. Delay. Frustration. Suspicion.

TEN OF SWORDS: Ruin. Tears and grief. Loss. Misfortune.

PAGE OF SWORDS: Confidence. Eagerness. Observation. Spying.

KNIGHT OF SWORDS: Conflict. Argument. Bravery. Leadership.

QUEEN OF SWORDS: Widowhood. Sterility. Privation. Undaunted spirit.

KING OF SWORDS: Authority. Wisdom. Superiority. Law and order.

Cups Suit.

ACE OF CUPS: Abundance in all things, especially love. Joy. Fertility.

TWO OF CUPS: Partnership; marriage; union. Love; friendship.

THREE OF CUPS: Success. Celebration. Fellowship. Joyfulness.

FOUR OF CUPS: Suspicion; doubt; uncertainty. Discontent. Jealousy.

FIVE OF CUPS: Partial loss. Momentary sadness. Change of plans.

SIX OF CUPS: Memories of the past. Promise of the future.

SEVEN OF CUPS: Abundance of ideas with nothing concrete. Dreams. Castles in the air.

EIGHT OF CUPS: A temporary parting. Journey to a strange land. Disappointment.

NINE OF CUPS: Material success. Freedom from want. Well-being. Satisfaction.

TEN OF CUPS: Happy family life. Success, not necessarily material. Honors.

PAGE OF CUPS: A birth. Receipt of news. Self-confidence. Promising start.

KNIGHT OF CUPS: Return in triumph. True love. Reciprocated love. An invitation.

QUEEN OF CUPS: Family and home. Happiness. Wife. Mother.

KING OF CUPS: Justice. Honor. Intelligence and learning. Authority.

Pentacles Suit.

ACE OF PENTACLES: Contentment in all things. Attainment.

TWO OF PENTACLES: Worry. Doubt; uncertainty. Juggling of affairs and finances.

THREE OF PENTACLES: Skills. Success. Trade. Arts and Crafts. Success in business.

FOUR OF PENTACLES: Settled business or home life. Few worries. Satisfaction.

FIVE OF PENTACLES: Want and poverty. Loneliness. Sudden loss.

SIX OF PENTACLES: Abundance. Material wealth and to spare. Gifts. Legacies.

SEVEN OF PENTACLES: Reward for work done. Gradual growth. Satisfaction in work done.

EIGHT OF PENTACLES: Craftsmanship. Work amply rewarded. Skill. Employment.

NINE OF PENTACLES: Leisure. Freedom from want. Sport and recreation. Vacation.

TEN OF PENTACLES: Established family or business. Investments. Legacies.

PAGE OF PENTACLES: Ambition. Messages. Longing for travel.

KNIGHT OF PENTACLES: Adventurer. Soldier. Materially minded. Gambler.

QUEEN OF PENTACLES: Intellectual. Kindness. Security. Generosity.

KING OF PENTACLES: Conceit. Pomposity. Inheritance. Success through gambling.

Of all the above meanings there is a slightly different interpretation possible should the card turn up reversed, i.e. upside-down. In the Major Arcana this usually indicates that the meaning as given above will be reversed. For example, Number 7—The Chariot, right way up means triumph and conquest. Reversed, however, it means defeat. Number 17—The Star; right way up means a change for the better, hope and promise for the future. Reversed it means a change for the worse, frustration; hopes not fulfilled. The Minor Arcana is not quite so opposite in its meaning when reversed. For example, the Two of Wands means fortunes and riches the right way up. Yet reversed it means comfort and adequacy. The Page of Pentacles means a longing to travel; while reversed it means a journey, wanted or not.

There are other methods of reading the Tarot; other

layouts that may be used. The Ancient Celtic method is probably the easiest and most convenient layout for the beginner. All should be tried, however, before you decide which you like best.

BIBLIOGRAPHY

I hope that the preceding articles have whetted your appetite for more of at least one aspect of the occult. In a book of this size it is obviously impossible to deal fully with all the subjects. I now list, therefore, a few of the books which will deal further with what I have introduced. They, in their turn, will contain lists of other books on their subjects. Start your trail here :

ASTRAL PROJECTION

Crookall, Robert *The Study and Practice of Astral Projection* Aquarian, London 1960
    Events on the Threshold of the After-Life Theosophical Pubs. 1966
Fox, Oliver *Astral Projection* Translantic Book Service 1962
Muldoon, S & Carrington H. *The Projection of the Astral Body* Rider, London 1968
"Ophiel" *The Art and Practice of Astral Projection* Llewellyn, Minn. 1966
"Yram" *Astral Projection*, Aquarian Press, London 1962

ASTROLOGY

Adams, E. *Astrology for Everyone* Transatlantic Book Service 1960
American Fed. of Astrologers *Basic Principles of Astrology* Llewellyn, Minn. 1962
Eisler, R. *The Royal Art of Astrology* London 1946
George, Llewellyn *Practical Astrology for Everybody* Llewellyn, Minn. 1966
Hone, M. E. *The Modern Text Book of Astrology* Fowler, London 1955
MacNeice, Louis *Astrology* Spring Books, London 1967

AUTOMATIC WRITING

Prince, W. F. *The Case of Patience Worth* Transatlantic Book Service 1964

Xavier, F. C. & Vieira, W. *The World of the Spirit* Philosophical Library, New York 1966

BLACK MAGIC

Baldick, R. *Life of J.-K. Huysmans* Clarendon Press, Oxford 1955

Crowley, A. *Magick in Theory and Practise* Wehman, New Jersey 1962

Huysmans, J.-K. *Down There (La Bas)* Transatlantic Book Service 1958

Rhodes, H. T. P. *The Satanic Mass* Arrow Books, London 1965

CEREMONIAL MAGIC

Burland, C. A. *The Magical Arts* Barker, London, 1966

Butler, E. M. *Ritual Magic* Hogarth Press, London 1949

Cavendish, R. *The Black Arts* Routledge, Kegan Paul, London 1967

Mathers, D. L. M. *The Key of Solomon the King* Kegan Paul 1909
The Book of Sacred Magic of Abra-Melin the Mage De Laurence, Chicago 1932

Shah, S. Idries *The Secret Lore of Magic* Muller 1957

Waite, A. E. *Ceremonial Magic* Transatlantic Book Service 1961

DIVINATION

Baughan, R. *The Influence of the Stars* London 1904

de Givry, G. *A Pictorial Anthology of Witchcraft, Magic and Alchemy* Transatlantic Book Service, London 1958

Kunz, G. F. *The Magic of Jewels and Charms* Lippincott, Pa. 1915

Miall, A. M. *Complete Fortune Telling* C. A. Pearson, London 1967

Randolph, V. *Ozark Superstitions* Dover/Constable, London 1969

Showers, P. *Fortune Telling for Fun and Profit* A. & C. Black, London 1967

DIVINING ROD

Roberts, Kenneth *Henry Gross and his Dowsing Rod* Collins, London 1931

Roberts, Kenneth *The Seventh Sense* Collins, London
Water Unlimited Collins 1928

Shannon, E. *Water Witching* Shannon, New Mexico 1967

ECTOPLASM

Flammarion, C. *Mysterious Psychic Forces* Unwin, London 1907

ESP

Barton, W. G. Ed. *Canada's Psi Century* Metaphysical Soc. of Canada 1967

Dingwall, E. & Langdon-Davies, J. *The Unknown—Is It Nearer?* New English Library, London 1967

Ebon, M. Ed. *True Experiences in Telepathy* New English Library, London 1967

Rhine, J. B. *New Frontiers of the Mind* H. A. Humphrey, London 1967

New World of the Mind Faber, London 1954

Rhine, Louisa *E.S.P. in Life and Lab.* Collier-Macmillan, London 1968

Sidgwick *Phantasms of the Living* Transatlantic Book Service 1962

Spraggett, A. *The Unexplained* New English Library, London 1967

Steiger, Brad. *ESP—Your Sixth Sense* Tandem Books, London 1967

HAUNTINGS

Bayless, R. *The Enigma of the Poltergeist* Ace Books, New York 1968

Saltzman, P. *Strange Spirits* Paperback Library, New York 1967

Steiger, Brad. *Strange Guests* Ace Books, New York 1966

The Unknown Popular Library, New York 1966

HYPNOSIS

Bernstein, M. *The Search for Bridey Murphy* Transatlantic Book Service, London 1965

Kelsey, D. & Grant, J. *Many Lifetimes* Gollancz, London 1969

Jensen, A. & Watkins, M. *Franz Anton Mesmer—Physician Extraordinaire* Garrett, New York 1967

LeCron, L. M. *Eperimental Hypnosis* Macmillan, London 1952

Powers, M. *Practical Guide to Self-Hypnosis* Thorsons, London 1956

I CHING

Blofeld, J. *The Book of Change* Allen & Unwin, London 1967

Wilhelm, R. tr. *I Ching* Routledge, Kegan Paul, London 1962

MEDIUMS

Archer, F. *Exploring the Psychic* Transatlantic Book Service, London 1967

Burton, J. *Heyday of a Wizard* Harrap, London 1948

Feilding, E. *Sittings With Eusapia Palladino* Heffer, London 1969

Ford, A. *Nothing So Strange* Harper & Row, New York 1958

Garrett, E. J. *Adventures in the Supernormal* Garrett, New York 1958

Wavell, S., Butt, A. & Epton, N. *Trances* Allen & Unwin, London 1967

NUMEROLOGY

Cheasley, C. W. *Numerology* Rider, London 1926

Cheiro *Cheiro's Book of Numbers* Corgi Books, London 1968

Lopez, V. *Numerology* Citadel Press, New York 1961

Adams, C. W. P. *Numerology for Everybody* Transatlantic Book Service, London 1940

PALMISTRY

Bryden, Dean *Palmistry for Pleasure* Sully, New York 1926

Hamon, Louis *Cheiro's Guide to the Hand* Wehman, New Jersey 1966

Van Alen, R. *You and Your Hand* Collins, London 1948
Wehman *Practical Palmistry* Wehman, New Jersey 1949

PSYCHOMETRY

Pagenstecher, G. *Past Events Seership* Proceedings American Soc. for Psychical Research, v.16, 1923
Puharich, A. *The Sacred Mushroom* Gollancz, London 1960
Solomon, H. Ed. *Studies in Item Analysis and Prediction* Cambridge Univ. Press 1961
Spraggett, A. *The Unexplained* New English Library, London 1967

RADIESTHESIA

Copen, B. *The Modern Prospector* Copen, England
Dietrich, C. *Pendulum Diagnosis* Copen, England
Mermet, Abbé *Principles and Practice of Radiesthesia* V. Stuart, London 1959
Wethered, V. *The Practice of Medical Radiesthesia* Fowler, London 1967

SCRYING

Besterman, T. *Crystal-Gazing* Rider, London 1924
"Velma" *My Mysteries and My Story* J. Long, London 1929

SPIRIT PHOTOGRAPHY

Eisenbud, J. *The World of Ted Serios* Jonathan Cape, London 1968
Los Angeles Times Wednesday February 3rd, 1932

TAROT

Case, P. F. *The Tarot* L. Fowler, London 1969

Gray, E. *The Tarot Revealed* Bodley Head, London 1958

Mathers, S. L. *The Tarot* Wehman, New Jersey 1966

Rakoczi, B. I. *The Painted Caravan* Lawrence, London 1954

Waite, A. E. *The Pictorial Guide to the Tarot* Rider, London 1922

QUEEN VICTORIA PRESS

Fiction by Raymond Buckland

A MISTAKE THROUGH THE HEART Book Three of the
Bram Stoker mysteries (Books One and Two were
published by Penguin/Random House's Berkley Prime
Crime imprint)

CHURCHILL'S SECRET SPY WWII espionage novel

THE PENNY COURT ENQUIRERS Victorian mystery series
    ONE CLUE AT A TIME Book One
    THE NOBLE SAVAGE Book Two
    DEADLY SPIRIT Book Three

OUT OF THIS WORLD science fiction short story collection

PARANORMAL POETRY A chapbook of poetry, strange and
unusual

In preparation:
  THE WIITIKO INHERITANCE
  THE SECRET LIFE OF MISS EMMELINE CROMWELL

Non-fiction by Raymond Buckland

WITCHCRAFT REVEALED An examination of Witchcraft
and Wicca

OUIJA CONNECTION TO SPIRIT The Talking Board and
how to contact the Spirit World

PARANORMAL PRIMER "How-to" on many popular metaphysical practices

HERE IS THE OCCULT An introduction to the wide world
of the paranormal

In preparation:
  THE BOOK OF ALCHEMY
  PSYCHIC WORLD SECRETS
  ANATOMY OF THE PARANORMAL

Fiction by Eileen Lizzie Wells

FLETCHER'S FOLLY A Gothic romance mystery

In preparation:
THE POSTMISTRESS MYSTERIES
DESIGNING WOMEN